DATE DUE

DEC 23 03			

Immigration

Opposing Viewpoints®

OTHER BOOKS OF RELATED INTEREST

OPPOSING VIEWPOINTS SERIES

American Foreign Policy
Central America
Culture Wars
Discrimination
Human Rights
Illegal Immigration
Interracial America
The New World Order
Population
Race Relations
Social Justice
The Third World
Welfare

CURRENT CONTROVERSIES SERIES

Illegal Immigration
Minorities
Nationalism and Ethnic Conflict
Racism

AT ISSUE SERIES

Ethnic Conflict
Immigration Policy

Immigration

Opposing Viewpoints®

David L. Bender, *Publisher*

Bruno Leone, *Executive Editor*

Brenda Stalcup, *Managing Editor*

Scott Barbour, *Senior Editor*

Tamara L. Roleff, *Book Editor*

OPPOSING
VIEWPOINTS®
SERIES

Greenhaven Press, Inc., San Diego, California

Cover photo: Sandra Baker, Gamma Liaison

Library of Congress Cataloging-in-Publication Data

Immigration : opposing viewpoints / Tamara L. Roleff, book editor.
    p.   cm. — (Opposing viewpoints series)
    Includes bibliographical references and index.
    ISBN 1-56510-799-3 (hbk. : alk. paper). — ISBN 1-56510-798-5
(pbk. : alk. paper)
    1. United States—Emigration and immigration. 2. Immigrants—
United States. 3. United States—Emigration and immigration—
Government policy. I. Roleff, Tamara L., 1959– . II. Series: Opposing viewpoints series (Unnumbered)
JV6465.U6I46 1998
325.73—dc21
                                               98-5034
                                                CIP

Greenhaven Press, Inc., P.O. Box 289009
San Diego, CA 92198-9009

"CONGRESS SHALL MAKE NO LAW...ABRIDGING THE FREEDOM OF SPEECH, OR OF THE PRESS."

First Amendment to the U.S. Constitution

The basic foundation of our democracy is the First Amendment guarantee of freedom of expression. The Opposing Viewpoints Series is dedicated to the concept of this basic freedom and the idea that it is more important to practice it than to enshrine it.

CONTENTS

WHY CONSIDER OPPOSING VIEWPOINTS?

"The only way in which a human being can make some approach to knowing the whole of a subject is by hearing what can be said about it by persons of every variety of opinion and studying all modes in which it can be looked at by every character of mind. No wise man ever acquired his wisdom in any mode but this."

John Stuart Mill

In our media-intensive culture it is not difficult to find differing opinions. Thousands of newspapers and magazines and dozens of radio and television talk shows resound with differing points of view. The difficulty lies in deciding which opinion to agree with and which "experts" seem the most credible. The more inundated we become with differing opinions and claims, the more essential it is to hone critical reading and thinking skills to evaluate these ideas. Opposing Viewpoints books address this problem directly by presenting stimulating debates that can be used to enhance and teach these skills. The varied opinions contained in each book examine many different aspects of a single issue. While examining these conveniently edited opposing views, readers can develop critical thinking skills such as the ability to compare and contrast authors' credibility, facts, argumentation styles, use of persuasive techniques, and other stylistic tools. In short, the Opposing Viewpoints Series is an ideal way to attain the higher-level thinking and reading skills so essential in a culture of diverse and contradictory opinions.

In addition to providing a tool for critical thinking, Opposing Viewpoints books challenge readers to question their own strongly held opinions and assumptions. Most people form their opinions on the basis of upbringing, peer pressure, and personal, cultural, or professional bias. By reading carefully balanced opposing views, readers must directly confront new ideas as well as the opinions of those with whom they disagree. This is not to simplistically argue that everyone who reads opposing views will—or should—change his or her opinion. Instead, the series enhances readers' understanding of their own views by encouraging confrontation with opposing ideas. Careful examination of others' views can lead to the readers' understanding of the logical inconsistencies in their own opinions, perspective on why they hold an opinion, and the consideration of the possibility that their opinion requires further evaluation.

EVALUATING OTHER OPINIONS

To ensure that this type of examination occurs, Opposing Viewpoints books present all types of opinions. Prominent spokespeople on different sides of each issue as well as well-known professionals from many disciplines challenge the reader. An additional goal of the series is to provide a forum for other, less known, or even unpopular viewpoints. The opinion of an ordinary person who has had to make the decision to cut off life support from a terminally ill relative, for example, may be just as valuable and provide just as much insight as a medical ethicist's professional opinion. The editors have two additional purposes in including these less known views. One, the editors encourage readers to respect others' opinions—even when not enhanced by professional credibility. It is only by reading or listening to and objectively evaluating others' ideas that one can determine whether they are worthy of consideration. Two, the inclusion of such viewpoints encourages the important critical thinking skill of objectively evaluating an author's credentials and bias. This evaluation will illuminate an author's reasons for taking a particular stance on an issue and will aid in readers' evaluation of the author's ideas.

As series editors of the Opposing Viewpoints Series, it is our hope that these books will give readers a deeper understanding of the issues debated and an appreciation of the complexity of even seemingly simple issues when good and honest people disagree. This awareness is particularly important in a democratic society such as ours in which people enter into public debate to determine the common good. Those with whom one disagrees should not be regarded as enemies but rather as people whose views deserve careful examination and may shed light on one's own.

Thomas Jefferson once said that "difference of opinion leads to inquiry, and inquiry to truth." Jefferson, a broadly educated man, argued that "if a nation expects to be ignorant and free . . . it expects what never was and never will be." As individuals and as a nation, it is imperative that we consider the opinions of others and examine them with skill and discernment. The Opposing Viewpoints Series is intended to help readers achieve this goal.

David L. Bender & Bruno Leone,
Series Editors

Greenhaven Press anthologies primarily consist of previously published material taken from a variety of sources, including periodicals, books, scholarly journals, newspapers, government documents, and position papers from private and public organizations. These original sources are often edited for length and to ensure their accessibility for a young adult audience. The anthology editors also change the original titles of these works in order to clearly present the main thesis of each viewpoint and to explicitly indicate the opinion presented in the viewpoint. These alterations are made in consideration of both the reading and comprehension levels of a young adult audience. Every effort is made to ensure that Greenhaven Press accurately reflects the original intent of the authors included in this anthology.

INTRODUCTION

"Immigration constitutes a primary source of vitality and renewal in our society."
— Doris Meissner, Forum for Applied Research
and Public Policy, Fall 1995

"Immigration is a luxury, not a necessity."
Peter Brimelow, Alien Nation, 1995

From a population of slightly less than 4 million at the time of the first census in 1790, the United States grew to 106 million by the 1920 census. Immigrants accounted for approximately 14 million of the population by then, with about 1 million new immigrants—nearly all of them European—arriving every year. Responding to concerns about the high number of immigrants arriving in the United States, Congress passed the Quota Act in 1921, which reduced the number of immigrants permitted into the country to 360,000 per year. Three years later, another immigration act introduced the "national origins" system, which limited the number of immigrants from specific countries to the proportion that had been admitted to the United States in 1910. No limits were placed on the number of European immigrants from England, Scandinavia, Germany, and France, but immigration from other European nations, Asia, and Africa was restricted. For example, just under 154,000 immigrants from Asian countries were permitted into the United States each year.

The 1965 Immigration Act made a dramatic difference in the makeup and number of immigrants to the United States. Although the act continued the setting of limits on the number of immigrants who could enter the United States from particular countries, it established the "family preference" rule, in which relatives of immigrants who were U.S. citizens were exempt from the quotas. Under the 1965 Immigration Act, Latin American and Asian countries still had a relatively low proportion of visas available to immigrants, but due to the family preference system, it was not long before these countries contributed a substantial portion of America's new immigrants. By 1990, 44 percent of America's legal immigrants were from Latin America and the Caribbean and 36 percent came from Asia. Less than 15 percent were from Europe.

Until 1921, illegal immigration was not a serious problem because almost anyone could enter the United States legally (the few exceptions were criminals, the sick, and those who could not support themselves). But with legal access to America now restricted by quotas, many immigrants took the risks of entering the country illegally through Canada or Mexico. Illegal immigration of migrant workers also increased dramatically after the 1965 Immigration Act canceled the *Bracero* program, which since the 1940s had allowed Mexicans to work in the fields of California and Texas for short periods of time. In one of its first serious attempts to control illegal immigration, Congress passed the 1986 Immigration Reform and Control Act (IRCA). The act had two parts: It provided amnesty to illegal immigrants who could prove they met certain requirements for living or working in the United States, and it sanctioned employers for hiring illegal aliens.

Most experts agree, however, that IRCA has had little effect in reducing illegal immigration. According to the Immigration and Naturalization Service (INS), 200,000 to 300,000 of the 1 million immigrants who enter the United States every year are illegal immigrants. Many people believe that America cannot continue to absorb so many immigrants—legal or illegal—without adversely affecting the economy. Peter Brimelow writes in *Alien Nation* that 90 percent of immigrants during the 1990s were from Third World countries and had lower job skill levels than native Americans. The presence of immigrants in the labor pool has an adverse effect on wages, Brimelow maintains, because employers will pay, and immigrants will accept, lower pay for low-skill jobs. He writes that the "national income *per capita* will fall—because those wages are far below the national average." The immigrants' low job skills are also directly responsible for a 50 percent decline in real wages for American high school dropouts, asserts David Jaeger, an economist at the Bureau of Labor Statistics. Furthermore, immigration critics contend that because immigrants are willing to work for less pay than native Americans, many Americans lose their jobs to immigrants.

Some politicians and economists charge that not only are immigrants forcing Americans out of their jobs, but immigrants are increasingly becoming a burden on those Americans who manage to keep their jobs. Federal law prohibits immigrants—legal or illegal—from depending on welfare or social services to support themselves. Despite this legislation, 21 percent of immigrants receive some form of subsidy by American taxpayers, according to social scientists. For example, a study by Robert Rector of the Heritage Foundation estimates that providing Medicaid to noncitizens will cost U.S. taxpayers an average of $2,000 each per year. In addition, critics contend that Supplemental Security Income (SSI), originally intended to financially assist elderly and disabled Americans, has become a retirement pension for 30 percent of elderly noncitizen immigrants.

Supporters of immigration argue that these fears about immigrants are baseless. According to Julian L. Simon, author of *The Economics of Immigration*, immigrants help the economy expand. He writes that "immigration does not exacerbate unemployment. . . . Immigrants not only take jobs, but also create them. Their purchases increase the demand for labor, leading to new hires roughly equal in number to the immigrant workers." Furthermore, advocates maintain, work performed by immigrants increases America's economic growth between $6 billion and $18 billion per year. Peter Salins, author of *Assimilation, American Style*, points out that immigration has had an extremely positive effect on San Diego, California. Over 20 percent of San Diegans are foreign-born, he asserts, yet the local economy has a low unemployment rate and is supported by high-tech industries. In fact, he concludes, cities such as Miami, Los Angeles, El Paso, New York, and Chicago—all of which have high immigration rates—have lower unemployment rates, lower welfare dependency, and bustling economies compared with Pittsburgh, Buffalo, Cleveland, Detroit, and St. Louis—all cities with low immigration rates.

Immigration advocates further contend that immigrants do not come to the United States in order to receive welfare payments; they come because they want to work. Moreover, they note that federal law prohibits immigrants from receiving welfare payments or public assistance for the first three to five years of residence. In fact, advocates point out, most immigrants arrive in the United States when they are young and healthy with a long working life ahead of them, and these immigrants actually help to subsidize the Social Security benefits of older Americans. Therefore, these advocates conclude, the benefits of immigration outweigh any negative effects.

The debate over immigration concerns more than economics and policies. Since the nation's founding, the United States has been a country of immigrants; the image of America welcoming the huddled masses to its shores is an integral part of how Americans view themselves and their country. *Immigration: Opposing Viewpoints* examines the issues inherent in legal and illegal immigration in the following chapters: Historical Debate: Should Immigration Be Restricted? Is Immigration a Problem for the United States? How Can Illegal Immigration Be Controlled? How Should U.S. Immigration Policy Be Reformed? The authors in this anthology explore the continuing ambivalence about immigration and America's vision of itself as the keeper of the golden door.

CHAPTER 1

HISTORICAL DEBATE: SHOULD IMMIGRATION BE RESTRICTED?

CHAPTER PREFACE

The debate over immigration is as old as the United States itself. "Despite the fact that almost all of us are immigrants or descendants of immigrants," writes immigration scholar George J. Borjas, "American history is characterized by a never-ending debate over when to pull the ladder in." Each wave of new immigrants—Irish in the 1840s, Chinese in the 1870s, Italians at the turn of the twentieth century, Cubans in the 1960s, Southeast Asians in the 1970s, and others—has sparked controversy among Americans whose immigrant forebears arrived earlier.

Many of the historical complaints about immigration are similar to those voiced today. The People's Party platform of 1882 proclaimed, "We condemn . . . the present system, which opens up our ports to the pauper and criminal classes of the world, and crowds out our wage earners." Borjas comments, "It seems that little has changed in the past hundred years. Today the same accusations are hurled at illegal aliens, at boat people originating in Southeast Asia and Cuba, and at other unskilled immigrants."

A prevalent theme throughout the historical immigration debate is racism. Many people believed that the latest immigrants to arrive in the United States were racially inferior to those who dominated previous immigration waves. Around the turn of the twentieth century, for example, Francis Walker, president of the Massachusetts Institute of Technology, described the incoming Italians, Greeks, Poles, and Russians as "beaten men from beaten races, representing the worst failures in the struggle for existence." Racism also played a major role in the immigration laws passed in the 1920s. These laws severely limited immigration from Asia, Latin America, and southern and eastern Europe. Their passage and eventual repeal in 1965 are major turning points in the history of U.S. immigration.

Examining past debates on immigration can shed light on present-day controversies. The viewpoints in this chapter present arguments on immigration at three different periods in American history.

> "The emigration of foreigners to this
> country is not only defensible on
> grounds of abstract justice ... [but]
> it has been in various ways highly
> beneficial to this country."

AMERICA SHOULD WELCOME IMMIGRATION (1845)

Thomas L. Nichols

Thomas L. Nichols (1815–1901) was a doctor, dietician, social
historian, and journalist. In the following viewpoint, written in
1845, he criticizes movements in the United States to restrict
immigration. He argues that prejudices against immigrants are
unfounded and that immigration has been beneficial to the
United States.

As you read, consider the following questions:

1. What racial beliefs does Nichols express concerning
   immigration?
2. How does the author characterize American immigrants?
3. According to Nichols, what is the worst thing that can be
   said about immigrants?

Thomas L. Nichols, "Lecture on Immigration and Right of Naturalization," in *Historical
Aspects of the Immigration Problem*, Edith Abbott, ed. New York: Arno Press, 1969.

The questions connected with emigration from Europe to America are interesting to both the old world and the new— are of importance to the present and future generations. They have more consequence than a charter or a state election; they involve the destinies of millions; they are connected with the progress of civilization, the rights of man, and providence of God!

EXAMINING PREJUDICES

I have examined this subject the more carefully, and speak upon it the more earnestly, because I have been to some extent, in former years, a partaker of the prejudices I have since learned to pity. A native of New England and a descendant of the puritans, I early imbibed, and to some extent promulgated, opinions of which reflection and experience have made me ashamed. . . .

Believing that the principles and practices of Native Americanism are wrong in themselves, and are doing wrong to those who are the objects of their persecution, justice and humanity require that their fallacy should be exposed, and their iniquity condemned. It may be unfortunate that the cause of the oppressed and persecuted, in opinion if not in action, has not fallen into other hands; yet, let me trust that the truth, even in mine, will prove mighty, prevailing from its own inherent power!

The right of man to emigrate from one country to another, is one which belongs to him by his own constitution and by every principle of justice. It is one which no law can alter, and no authority destroy. "Life, liberty, and the pursuit of happiness" are set down, in our Declaration of Independence, as among the self-evident, unalienable rights of man. If I have a right to live, I have also a right to what will support existence—food, clothing, and shelter. If then the country in which I reside, from a superabundant population, or any other cause, does not afford me these, my right to go from it to some other is self-evident and unquestionable. The right to live, then, supposes the right of emigration. . . .

The emigration of foreigners to this country is not only defensible on grounds of abstract justice—what we have no possible right to prevent, but . . . it has been in various ways highly beneficial to this country.

Emigration first peopled this hemisphere with civilized men. The first settlers of this continent had the same right to come here that belongs to the emigrant of yesterday—no better and no other. They came to improve their condition, to escape from oppression, to enjoy freedom—for the same, or similar, reasons as now prevail. And so far as they violated no private rights, so long as they obtained their lands by fair purchase, or took possession of those which were unclaimed and uncultivated, the highly respectable natives whom the first settlers found here had no right to make any objections. The peopling of this continent with civilized men, the cultivation of the earth, the various processes of productive labor, for the happiness of man, all tend to "the greatest good of the greatest number," and carry out the evident design of Nature or Providence in the formation of the earth and its inhabitants.

LET THEM COME

The poor flock to our shores to escape from a state of penury, which cannot be relieved by toil in their own native land. The man of enterprise comes, to avail himself of the advantages afforded by a wider and more varied field for the exercise of his industry and talents; and the oppressed of every land, thirsting for deliverance from the paralyzing effects of unjust institutions, come to enjoy the blessings of a government which secures life, liberty, and the pursuit of happiness to all its constituents. Let them come. They will convert our waste lands into fruitful fields, vineyards, and gardens; construct works of public improvement; build up and establish manufactures; and open our rich mines of coal, of iron, of lead, and of copper. And more than all, they will be the means of augmenting our commerce, and aiding us in extending the influence of our political, social, and religious institutions throughout the earth.

Western Journal, vol. 6, 1851.

Emigration from various countries in Europe to America, producing a mixture of races, has had, and is still having, the most important influence upon the destinies of the human race. It is a principle, laid down by every physiologist, and proved by abundant observation, that man, like other animals, is improved and brought to its highest perfection by an intermingling of the blood and qualities of various races. That nations and families deteriorate from an opposite course has been observed in all ages. The great physiological reason why Americans are superior to other nations in freedom, intelligence, and enterprise, is because that they are the offspring of the greatest intermingling of races. The mingled blood of England has given her predominance over several nations of Europe in these very qualities, and a newer infusion, with favorable circumstances of climate, position, and institutions, has rendered Americans still superior. The Yankees of New England would never have shown those qualities for which they have been distinguished in war and peace throughout the world had there not been mingled with the puritan English, the calculating Scotch, the warm hearted Irish, the gay and chivalric French, the steady persevering Dutch, and the transcendental Germans, for all these nations contributed to make up the New England character, before the Revolution, and ever since to influence that of the whole American people.

It is not too much to assert that in the order of Providence this vast and fertile continent was reserved for this great destiny; to be the scene of this mingling of the finest European races, and consequently of the highest condition of human intelligence, freedom, and happiness; for I look upon this mixture of the blood and qualities of various nations, and its continual infusion, as absolutely requisite to the perfection of humanity. . . . Continual emigration, and a constant mixing of the blood of different races, is highly conducive to physical and mental superiority.

ECONOMIC BENEFITS

This country has been continually benefited by the immense amount of capital brought hither by emigrants. There are very few who arrive upon our shores without some little store of wealth, the hoard of years of industry. Small as these means may be in each case, they amount to millions in the aggregate, and every dollar is so much added to the wealth of the country, to be reckoned at compound interest from the time of its arrival, nor are these sums like our European loans, which we must pay back, both principal and interest. Within a few years, especially, and more or less at all periods, men of great wealth have been among the emigrants driven from Europe, by religious oppression or political revolutions. Vast sums have also fallen to emigrants and their descendants by inheritance, for every few days we read in the papers of some poor foreigner, or descendant of foreigners, as are we all, becoming the heir of a princely fortune, which in most cases, is added to the wealth of his adopted country. Besides this, capital naturally follows labor, and it flows upon this country in a constant current, by the laws of trade.

But it is not money alone that adds to the wealth of a country but every day's productive labor is to be added to its accumulating capital. Every house built, every canal dug, every railroad graded, has added so much to the actual wealth of society; and who have built more houses, dug more canals, or graded more railroads, than the hardy Irishmen? I hardly know how our great national works could have been carried on without them then; while every pair of sturdy arms has added to our national

wealth, every hungry mouth has been a home market for our
agriculture, and every broad shoulder has been clothed with our
manufactures.

RECEIVE THEM AS FRIENDS

Let us by no means join in the popular outcry against foreigners
coming to our country, and partaking of its privileges. They will
come, whether we will or no; and is it wise to meet them with
inhospitality, and thus turn their hearts against us? Let us rather
receive them as friends, and give them welcome to our country.
Let us rather say, "The harvest before us is indeed great, and the
laborers are few: come, go with us, and we will do thee good."
Our hills, and valleys, and rivers, stretch from ocean to ocean,
belting the entire continent of the New World; and over this rich
and boundless domain, Providence has poured the atmosphere
of liberty. Let these poor sufferers come and breathe it freely. Let
our country be the asylum of the oppressed of all lands. Let
those who come bent down with the weight of European tithes
and taxation, here throw off the load, and stand erect in freedom.

Samuel Griswold Goodrich, *Ireland and the Irish*, 1841.

From the very nature of the case, America gets from Europe
the most valuable of her population. Generally, those who come
here are the very ones whom a sensible man would select. Those
who are attached to monarchical and aristocratic institutions
stay at home where they can enjoy them. Those who lack energy
and enterprise can never make up their minds to leave their native land. It is the strong minded, the brave hearted, the free and
self-respecting, the enterprising and the intelligent, who break
away from all the ties of country and of home, and brave the
dangers of the ocean, in search of liberty and independence, for
themselves and for their children, on a distant continent; and it
is from this, among other causes, that the great mass of the
people of this country are distinguished for the very qualities
we should look for in emigrants. The same spirit which sent our
fathers across the ocean impels us over the Alleghenies, to the
valley of the Mississippi, and thence over the Rocky mountains
into Oregon.

INDEBTED TO IMMIGRANTS

For what are we not indebted to foreign emigration, since we
are all Europeans or their descendants? We cannot travel on one
of our steamboats without remembering that Robert Fulton was

the son of an Irishman. We cannot walk by St. Paul's churchyard without seeing the monuments which admiration and gratitude have erected to Emmet, and [Richard] Montgomery. Who of the thousands who every summer pass up and down our great thoroughfare, the North River, fails to catch at least a passing glimpse of the column erected to the memory of Thaddeus Kosciusko? I cannot forget that only last night a portion of our citizens celebrated with joyous festivities the birthday of the son of Irish emigrants, I mean the Hero of New Orleans [Andrew Jackson]!

Who speaks contemptuously of Alexander Hamilton as a foreigner, because he was born in one of the West India Islands? Who at this day will question the worth or patriotism of Albert Gallatin, because he first opened his eyes among the Alps of Switzerland—though, in fact, this was brought up and urged against him, when he was appointed special minister to Russia by James Madison. What New Yorker applies the epithet of "degraded foreigner" to the German immigrant, John Jacob Astor, a man who has spread his canvas on every sea, drawn to his adopted land the wealth of every clime, and given us, it may be, our best claim to vast territories!

Who would have banished the Frenchman, Stephen Girard, who, after accumulating vast wealth from foreign commerce, endowed with it magnificent institutions for education in his adopted land? So might I go on for hours, citing individual examples of benefits derived by this country from foreign immigration. . . .

The "Harms" of Immigration

I have enumerated some of the advantages which such emigration has given to America. Let us now very carefully inquire, whether there is danger of any injury arising from these causes, at all proportionable to the palpable good.

"Our country is in danger," is the cry of Nativism. During my brief existence I have seen this country on the very verge of ruin a considerable number of times. It is always in the most imminent peril every four years; but, hitherto, the efforts of one party or the other have proved sufficient to rescue it, just in the latest gasp of its expiring agonies, and we have breathed more freely, when we have been assured that "the country's safe." Let us look steadily in the face of this new danger.

Are foreigners coming here to overturn our government? Those who came before the Revolution appear to have been generally favorable to Republican institutions. Those who have come here since have left friends, home, country, all that man naturally holds dearest, that they might live under a free government—they and their children. Is there common sense in the supposition that men would voluntarily set about destroying the very liberties they came so far to enjoy?

"But they lack intelligence," it is said. Are the immigrants of today less intelligent than those of fifty or a hundred years ago? Has Europe and the human race stood still all this time? . . . The facts of men preferring this country to any other, of their desire to live under its institutions, of their migration hither, indicate to my mind anything but a lack of proper intelligence and enterprise. It has been charged against foreigners, by a portion of the whig press, that they generally vote with the democratic party. Allowing this to be so, I think that those who reflect upon the policy of the two parties, from the time of John Adams down to that of Mayor Harper, will scarcely bring this up as the proof of a lack of intelligence!

The truth is, a foreigner who emigrates to this country comes here saying, "Where Liberty dwells, there is my country." He sees our free institutions in the strong light of contrast. The sun seems brighter, because he has come out of darkness. What we know by hearsay only of the superiority of our institutions, he knows by actual observation and experience. Hence it is that America has had no truer patriots—freedom no more enthusiastic admirers—the cause of liberty no more heroic defenders, than have been found among our adopted citizens. . . .

But if naturalized citizens of foreign birth had the disposition, they have not the power, to endanger our liberties, on account of their comparatively small and decreasing numbers. There appears to be a most extraordinary misapprehension upon this subject. To read one of our "Native" papers one might suppose that our country was becoming overrun by foreigners, and that there was real danger of their having a majority of votes. . . .

IMMIGRATION IS INSIGNIFICANT

There is a point beyond which immigration cannot be carried. It must be limited by the capacity of the vessels employed in bringing passengers, while our entire population goes on increasing in geometrical progression, so that in one century from now, we shall have a population of one hundred and sixty millions, but a few hundred thousands of whom at the utmost can be citizens of foreign birth. Thus it may be seen that foreign immigration is of very little account, beyond a certain period, in the population of a country, and at all times is an insignificant item. . . .

In the infancy of this country the firstborn native found himself among a whole colony of foreigners. Now, the foreigner finds himself surrounded by as great a disproportion of natives, and the native babe and newly landed foreigner have about the same amount, of either power or disposition, to endanger the country in which they have arrived; one, because he chose to come—the other because he could not help it.

I said the power or the disposition, for I have yet to learn that foreigners, whether German or Irish, English or French, are at all disposed to do an injury to the asylum which wisdom has prepared and valor won for the oppressed of all nations and religions. I appeal to the observation of every man in this community, whether the Germans and the Irish here, and throughout the country, are not as orderly, as industrious, as quiet, and in the habit of performing as well the common duties of citizens as the great mass of natives among us.

The worst thing that can be brought against any portion of our foreign population is that in many cases they are poor, and when they sink under labor and privation, they have no resources but the almshouse. Alas! shall the rich, for whom they have labored, the owners of the houses they have helped to build, refuse to treat them as kindly as they would their horses when incapable of further toil? Can they grudge them shelter from the storm, and a place where they may die in peace?

"The mighty tides of immigration
... bring to us not only different
languages, opinions, customs, and
principles, but hostile races,
religions, and interests."

AMERICA SHOULD DISCOURAGE IMMIGRATION (1849)

Garrett Davis

In the 1820s and 1830s the rate of immigration to the United States increased dramatically, with Ireland and Germany replacing Great Britain as the main source of immigrants. Many Americans became concerned about the potential negative effects of this increase in immigration. The following viewpoint is taken from an 1849 speech by Garrett Davis (1801–1872) in which he argues that immigrants endanger America. He contends that the United States should discourage immigration and should restrict immigrants' right to vote. Davis served as a U.S. senator and congressman for the state of Kentucky.

As you read, consider the following questions:

1. How does Davis describe America's newest immigrants?
2. What predictions does Davis make concerning Europe and the United States?
3. What connection does the author make concerning immigration and slavery?

Garrett Davis, speech delivered to the Convention to Revise the Constitution of Kentucky, December 15, 1849, in *Historical Aspects of the Immigration Problem*, Edith Abbott, ed. New York: Arno Press, 1969.

Why am I opposed to the encouragement of foreign immigration into our country, and disposed to apply any proper checks to it? Why do I propose to suspend to the foreigner, for twenty-one years after he shall have signified formally his intention to become a citizen of the United States, the right of suffrage, the birthright of no man but one native-born? It is because the mighty tides of immigration, each succeeding one increasing in volume, bring to us not only different languages, opinions, customs, and principles, but hostile races, religions, and interests, and the traditionary prejudices of generations with a large amount of the turbulence, disorganizing theories, pauperism, and demoralization of Europe in her redundant population thrown upon us. This multiform and dangerous evil exists and will continue, for "the cry is, Still they come!". . .

The most of those European immigrants, having been born and having lived in the ignorance and degradation of despotisms, without mental or moral culture, with but a vague consciousness of human rights, and no knowledge whatever of the principles of popular constitutional government, their interference in the political administration of our affairs, even when honestly intended, would be about as successful as that of the Indian in the arts and business of civilized private life; and when misdirected, as it would generally be, by bad and designing men, could be productive only of mischief, and from their numbers, of mighty mischief. The system inevitably and in the end will fatally depreciate, degrade, and demoralize the power which governs and rules our destinies.

I freely acknowledge that among such masses of immigrants there are men of noble intellect, of high cultivation, and of great moral worth; men every way adequate to the difficult task of free, popular, and constitutional government. But the number is lamentably small. There can be no contradistinction between them and the incompetent and vicious; and their admission would give no proper compensation, no adequate security against the latter if they, too, were allowed to share political sovereignty. The country could be governed just as wisely and as well by the native-born citizens alone, by which this baleful infusion would be wholly excluded. . . .

THE SITUATION IN EUROPE

This view of the subject is powerfully corroborated by a glance at the state of things in Europe. The aggregate population of that continent in 1807 was 183,000,000. Some years since it was reported to be 260,000,000 and now it is reasonably but little short of 283,000,000; showing an increase within a period of about forty years of 100,000,000. The area of Europe is but little more than that of the United States, and from its higher northern positions and greater proportion of sterile lands, has a less natural capability of sustaining population. All her western, southern, and middle states labor under one of the heaviest afflictions of nations—they have a redundant population. The German states have upward of 70,000,000, and Ireland 8,000,000; all Germany being not larger than three of our largest states, and Ireland being about the size of Kentucky. Daniel O'Connell, in 1843 reported 2,385,000 of the Irish people in a state of destitution. The annual increase of population in Germany and Ireland is in the aggregate near 2,000,000; and in all Europe it is near 7,000,000. Large masses of these people, in many countries, not only want the comforts of life, but its subsistence, its necessaries, and are literally starving. England, many of the German powers, Switzerland, and other governments, have put into operation extensive and well-arranged systems of emigrating and transporting to America their excess of population, and particularly the refuse, the pauper, the demoralized, and the criminal. Very many who come are stout and industrious, and go to labor steadily and thriftily. They send their friends in the old country true and glowing accounts of ours, and with it the means which they have garnered here to bring, too, those friends. Thus, immigration itself increases its means, and constantly adds to its swelling tides. Suppose some mighty convulsion of nature should loosen Europe, the smaller country, from her ocean-deep foundations, and drift her to our coast, would we be ready to take her teeming myriads to our fraternal embrace and give them equally our political sovereignty? If we did, in a few fleeting years where would be the noble Anglo-American race, where their priceless heritage of liberty, where their free constitution, where the best and brightest hopes of man? All would have perished! It is true all Europe is not coming to the United States, but much, too much of it, is; and a dangerous disproportion of the most ignorant and worst of it, without bringing us any territory for them; enough, if they go on increasing and to increase, and are to share with us our power, to bring about such a deplorable result. The question is, Shall they come and take possession of our country and our government, and rule us, or will we, who have the right, rule them and ourselves? I go openly, manfully, and perseveringly for the latter rule, and if it cannot be successfully asserted in all the United States, I am for taking measures to maintain it in Kentucky, and while we can. Now is the time—prevention is easier than cure.

A SURPLUS POPULATION

The governments of Europe know better than we do that they have a great excess of population. They feel more intensely its great and manifold evils, and for years they have been devising and applying correctives, which have all been mainly resolved into one—to drain off into America their surplus, and especially their destitute, demoralized, and vicious population. By doing so, they not only make more room and comfort for the residue, but they think—and with some truth—that they provide for their own security, and do something to avert explosions which might hurl kings from their thrones. . . .

IMMINENT PERIL

It is an incontrovertible truth that the civil institutions of the United States of America have been seriously affected, and that they now stand in imminent peril from the rapid and enormous increase of the body of residents of foreign birth, imbued with foreign feelings, and of an ignorant and immoral character, who receive, under the present lax and unreasonable laws of naturalization, the elective franchise and the right of eligibility to political office.

Declaration of the Native American National Convention, July 4, 1845.

We have a country of vast extent, with a great variety of climate, soil, production, industry, and pursuit. Competing interests and sectional questions are a natural and fruitful source of jealousies, discords, and factions. We have about four millions of slaves, and the slaveholding and free states are nearly equally divided in number, but the population of the latter greatly preponderating, and every portion of it deeply imbued with inflexible hostility to slavery as an institution. Even now conflict of opinion and passion of the two great sections of the Union upon the subject of slavery is threatening to rend this Union, and change confederated states and one people into hostile and warring powers. Cession [by Mexico of the Upper California, Utah, and New Mexico territories] has recently given to us considerable numbers of the Spanish race, and a greatly increasing immigration is constantly pouring in upon us the hordes of Europe, with their hereditary national animosities, their discordant races, languages, and religious faiths, their ignorance and their pauperism, mixed up with a large amount of idleness, moral degradation, and crime; and all this "heterogeneous, discordant, distracted mass," to use Mr. Jefferson's language, "sharing with us the legislation" and the entire political sovereignty. . . .

Washington and Jefferson and their associates, though among the wisest and most far-seeing of mankind, could not but descry in the future many formidable difficulties and dangers, and thus be premonished to provide against them in fashioning our institutions. If they had foreseen the vast, the appalling increase of immigration upon us at the present, there can be no reasonable doubt that laws to naturalize the foreigners and to give up to them the country, its liberties, its destiny, would not have been authorized by the constitution. The danger, though great, is not wholly without remedy. We can do something if we do it quickly. The German and Slavonic races are combining in the state of New York to elect candidates of their own blood to Congress. This is the beginning of the conflict of races on a large scale, and it must, in the nature of things, continue and increase. It must be universal and severe in all the field of labor, between the native and the stranger, and from the myriads of foreign laborers coming to us, if it does not become a contest for bread and subsistence, wages will at least be brought down so low as to hold our native laborers and their families in hopeless poverty. They cannot adopt the habits of life and live upon the stinted meager supplies to which the foreigner will restrict himself, and which is bounteous plenty to what he has been accustomed in the old country. Already these results are taking place in many of the mechanic arts. Duty, patriotism, and wisdom all require us to protect the labor, and to keep up to a fair scale the wages of our native-born people as far as by laws and measures of public policy it can be done. The foreigner, too, is the natural foe of the slavery of our state. He is opposed to it by all his past associations, and when he comes to our state he sees 200,000 laborers of a totally different race to himself excluding him measurably from employment and wages. He hears a measure agitated to send these 200,000 competitors away. Their exodus will make room for him, his kindred and race, and create such a demand for labor, as he will reason it, to give him high wages. He goes naturally for the measure, and becomes an emancipationist. While the slave is with us, the foreigner will not crowd us, which will postpone to a long day the affliction of nations, an excess of population; the slaves away, the great tide of immigration will set in upon us, and precipitate upon our happy land this, the chief misery of most of the countries of Europe. Look at the myriads who are perpetually pouring into the northwestern states from the German hives—making large and exclusive settlements for themselves, which in a few years will number their thousands and tens of thousands, living in isolation; speaking a strange language, having alien manners, habits, opinions, and religious faiths, and a total ignorance of our political institutions; all handed down with German phlegm and inflexibility to their children through generations. In less than fifty years, northern Illinois, parts of Ohio, and Michigan, Wisconsin, Iowa, and Minnesota will be literally possessed by them; they will number millions and millions, and they will be essentially a distinct people, a nation within a nation, a new Germany. We can't keep these people wholly out, and ought not if we could; but we are getting more than our share of them. I wish they would turn their direction to South America, quite as good a portion of the world as our share of the hemisphere. They could there aid in bringing up the slothful and degenerate Spanish race; here their deplorable office is to pull us down. Our proud boast is that the Anglo-Saxon race is the first among all the world of man, and that we are a shoot from this noble stock; but how long will we be as things are progressing? In a few years, as a distinctive race, the Anglo-Americans will be as much lost to the world and its future history as the lost tribes of Israel. . . .

THE DANGERS OF FOREIGNERS

The rapid increase of any nation, by means of an influx of foreigners, is dangerous to the repose of that nation; especially if the number of emigrants bears any considerable proportion to the old inhabitants. Even if that proportion is very small, the tendency of the thing is injurious, unless the newcomers are more civilized and more virtuous, and have at the same time, the same ideas and feeling about government. But if they are more vicious, they will corrupt; if less industrious, they will promote idleness; if they have different ideas of government, they will contend; if the same, they will intrigue and interfere.

Samuel Whelpley, A Compend of History from the Earliest Times, Comprehending a General View of the Present State of the World, 1825.

No well-informed and observant man can look abroad over this widespread and blessed country without feeling deep anxiety for the future. Some elements of discord and disunion are even now in fearful action. Spread out to such a vast extent, filling up almost in geometrical progression with communities and colonies from many lands, various as Europe in personal and national characteristics, in opinions, in manners and customs, in tongues and religious faiths, in the traditions of the past, and the objects and the hopes of the future, the United States can, no more than Europe, become one homogeneous mass—one peaceful, united, harmonizing, all self-adhering people. When the country shall begin to teem with people, these jarring elements being brought into proximity, their repellent and explosive properties will begin to act with greater intensity; and then, if not before, will come the war of geographical sections, the war of races, and the most relentless of all wars, of hostile religions. This mournful catastrophe will have been greatly hastened by our immense expansion and our proclamation to all mankind to become a part of us.

"By restricting immigration we . . . will give to a large body of citizens a decent and comfortable standard of living."

RESTRICTIONS ON IMMIGRATION ARE NECESSARY (1913)

Frank Julian Warne

The late 1800s and early 1900s were peak years for immigration to the United States. Many of these immigrants came from southern and eastern Europe, and their arrival rekindled debates over immigration. Some Americans argued that these new arrivals were racially inferior, while others said immigrants took away jobs and depressed wages. The following viewpoint is excerpted from the book *The Immigrant Invasion* by Frank Julian Warne (1874–1948). Focusing on economics instead of race, Warne states that the influx of immigrants is creating a lower standard of living for all Americans. He maintains that the United States needs national legislation restricting immigration. An economist and author, Warne served as a special expert on immigrants for the 1910 U.S. Census.

As you read, consider the following questions:

1. What is the central issue of immigration, according to Warne?
2. How does the author respond to the argument that immigrants take jobs other people do not want?
3. What kinds of new laws on immigration does Warne propose?

Excerpted from *The Immigration Invasion* by Frank Julian Warne. New York: Dodd, Mead and Company. 1913.

D ifferent people studying and observing the immigration phenomenon do not always see the same thing—they receive different impressions from it. Sometimes the other view is apparent to their consciousness but usually their mind is so taken up with their own view that the other is of lesser significance.

Two Views of Immigration

One view of immigration is that which is conspicuous to the worker who has been and is being driven out of his position by the immigrant; to members of the labour union struggling to control this competition and to maintain their standard of living; to those who see the socially injurious and individually disastrous effects upon the American worker of this foreign stream of cheap labour; to those who know the pauperising effects of a low wage, long hours of work, and harsh conditions of employment; to those personally familiar with the poverty in many of our foreign "colonies"; to those acquainted with the congested slum districts in our large industrial centres and cities and the innumerable problems which they present; to those who long and strive for an early realisation of Industrial Democracy. . . .

The other view is seen, however, by those who believe that the immigrant is escaping from intolerable religious, racial, and political persecution and oppression; whose sympathies have been aroused by a knowledge of the adverse economic conditions of the masses of Europe; by those immigrants and their children already here who desire to have their loved ones join them; by producers and manufacturers seeking cheap labour; by those holding bonds and stocks in steamship companies receiving large revenues from the transportation of the immigrant; by those who see subjects of European despotism transformed into naturalised citizens of the American republic, with all that this implies for them and for their children.

The so-called good side of immigration is seen primarily from the viewpoint of the immigrant himself. Any perspective of immigration through the eyes of the alien must necessarily, as a rule, be an optimistic one. Although some of them are possibly worse off in the United States than if they had remained in their European home, at the same time the larger number improve their condition by coming to America. Let us admit, then, that immigration benefits the immigrant.

Thus are indicated two views of immigration. These opposite views are very rapidly dividing the American people into two camps or parties—those who favour a continuance of our present liberal policy and those who are striving to have laws passed that will further restrict immigration. The different groups are made up for the most part of well-intentioned people looking at identically the same national problem but who see entirely different aspects or effects. . . .

The Real Issue

Those who are desirous of settling the immigration question solely from the point of view of the best interests of the country are quite frequently sidetracked from the only real and fundamental argument into the discussion of relatively unimportant phases of it. The real objection to immigration at the present time lies not in the fact that Slavs and Italians and Greeks and Syrians instead of Irish and Germans and English are coming to the United States. Nor does it lie in the fact that the immigrants are or become paupers and criminals. The real objection has nothing to do with the composition of our immigration stream, nor with the characteristics of the individuals or races composing it. It is more than likely that the evils so prominent today would still exist if we had received the Slavs and Italians fifty years ago and were receiving the English and Irish and Germans at the present day.

The real objection to immigration lies in the changed conditions that have come about in the United States themselves. These conditions now dominate and control the tendencies that immigration manifests. At the present time they are giving to the country a surplus of cheap labour—a greater supply than our industries and manufacturing enterprises need. In consequence this over-supply has brought into play among our industrial toilers the great law of competition. This economic law is controlled by the more recent immigrant because of his immediate necessity to secure employment and his ability to sell his labour at a low price—to work for a low wage. Against the operation of this law the native worker and the earlier immigrant are unable to defend themselves. It is affecting detrimentally the standard of living of hundreds of thousands of workers—workers, too, who are also citizens, fathers, husbands.

Immigrants and Machines

But who will do the rough work that must be done if we cannot get the immigrant? asks the liberal immigrationist. And to clinch his argument he goes into raptures over the industrial characteristics of the immigrant and points out enthusiastically the important part the alien has played in America's material upbuilding.

Immigration tends to retard the invention and introduction of machinery which otherwise would do this rough work for us. It has prevented capital in our industries from giving the proper amount of attention to the increase and use of machines, says Professor John R. Commons in "Races and Immigrants in America." "The cigar-making machine cannot extensively be introduced on the Pacific coast because Chinese cheap labour makes the same cigars at less cost than the machines. High wages stimulate the invention and use of machinery and scientific processes, and it is machinery and science, more than mere hand labour, on which reliance must be placed to develop the natural resources of a country. But machinery and science cannot be as quickly introduced as cheap immigrant labour. . . . In the haste to get profits the immigrant is more desired than machinery."

As long as cheap labour is available this tendency will continue. Even in spite of the large supply of immigrants who work for a low wage, what has already been accomplished along the line of adapting machinery to do the rough work is but indicative of what would be done in this direction if immigration were restricted. . . .

U.S. IMMIGRATION HURTS OTHER COUNTRIES

When anyone suggests the restriction of immigration to those who believe in throwing open wide our gates to all the races of the world, the conclusion is immediately arrived at that the proposer has some personal feeling in the matter and that he is not in sympathy with the immigrant. As a matter of fact the restriction of immigration is herein suggested not alone from the point of view of the future political development of the United States, but also from that of the interest and welfare of the immigrant himself and his descendants. It is made in order to prevent them from becoming in the future an industrial slave class in America and to assist them in throwing off in their European homes the shackles which now bind them and are the primary cause of their securing there so little from an abundant world.

One of the strongest arguments in the past of the liberal immigrationist is that the downtrodden and oppressed of Europe are fleeing from intolerable economic, political, and religious conditions into a land of liberty and freedom which offers opportunities to all. It may be very much questioned if these immigrants are finding here the hoped-for escape from oppression and servitude and exploitation, for since the newer immigration began in the eighties there has come to dwell in America a horrible modern Frankenstein in the shape of the depressing conditions surrounding a vast majority of our industrial toilers. But even granting that the immigrants coming to us do better their condition, a very pertinent question is as to the effect the prevention of this immigration would have upon the countries from which it comes. If we grant that the immigrants are ablebodied, disposed to resent oppression and are striving to better their condition, are they not the very ones that should remain in their European homes and there through growing restlessness and increasing power change for the better the conditions from which they are fleeing? As it is now, instead of an improvement in those conditions the stronger and more able-bodied—the ones better able to cope with them and improve them—are running away and leaving behind the less able and weaker members, who continue to live under the intolerable conditions.

UNITE TO REDUCE IMMIGRATION

It is the duty of all Americans from Maine to Texas and from Washington to Florida to forget the dissensions of the past and unite in an effort to reduce immigration to the lowest possible point or stop it altogether, and to compel the foreigners now here either to accept our traditions and ideals or else to return to the land from which they came, by deportation or otherwise.

Madison Grant, *The Alien in Our Midst*, 1930.

If immigration to the United States were stopped one would not likely be far wrong in prophesying that either one of two things would happen in these European countries: Either a voluntary remedying by the European Governments themselves of political, religious, and economic evils, or else those countries would soon be confronted by revolutions springing from this unrest of the people which now finds an escape through emigration to the United States. . . . Pent up discontent, unrelieved by emigration, would burst its bounds to the betterment of the general social conditions of the European masses.

Another phase of this same aspect of immigration is the fact that indirectly the United States which, if it stands for anything, stands in opposition to nearly all that is represented by the European form of government—this country, to a considerable extent, helps to keep in power these very governments against which it is a living protest. This is done in one way through the enormous sums of money that immigrants in the United States send each year to the European countries.

It is estimated that from two hundred to two hundred and fifty million dollars are sent abroad annually to the more important European countries by the foreign born in the United States. Part of this enormous sum finds its way by direct and indirect taxation into the coffers of the Government and the Bureaucracy and thus tends to support and continue them in power. When this fact is kept in mind—the fact that nearly two hundred and fifty million dollars are sent abroad each year by immigrants in the United States—it is an argument that answers thoroughly the claim of large employers of labour that immigration is an advantage to the country in that it brings to us annually through the immigrant nearly $25,000,000. The fact is that an amount nine times greater than that brought in is sent out of the country each year by the immigrant. . . .

NEEDED: MORE RESTRICTIONS

Virtually all objection or opposition to any suggestion as to immigration restriction comes from the immigrant races themselves. As for the attitude of the native, he seems for the greater part to be apathetic when it comes to taking some practical action to remedy conditions, although his grumbling and open opposition is becoming louder than ever before.

Our present statutes, except as they relate to labourers brought in under contract, exclude only such manifestly undesirable persons as idiots, the insane, paupers, immigrants likely to become a public charge, those with loathsome or dangerous contagious diseases, persons whose physical or mental defects prevent them from earning a living, convicted criminals, prostitutes, and the like. Even a strict enforcement of these laws makes it possible to keep out only the poorest and worst elements in these groups who come here.

Referring to the fact that certain undesirable immigrants are not being reached by the present laws the Commissioner of Immigration at Ellis Island, Mr. William Williams, says:

> We have no statutes excluding those whose economic condition is so low that their competition tends to reduce the standard of our wage worker, nor those who flock to the congested districts of our large cities where their presence may not be needed, in place of going to the country districts where immigrants of the right type are needed. As far back as 1901 reference was made by President Roosevelt in his annual message to Congress to those foreign labourers who 'represent a standard of living so depressed that they can undersell our men in the labour market and drag them to a lower level,' and it was recommended that

'all persons should be excluded who are below a certain standard of economic fitness to enter our industrial fields as competitors with American labourers.' There are no laws under which aliens of the class described can be kept out unless they happen to fall within one of the classes now excluded by statutes (as they sometimes do); and yet organised forces are at work, principally on the other side of the ocean, to induce many to come here whose standards of living are so low that it is detrimental to the best interests of the country that the American labourers should be compelled to compete with them.

To regulate, and this means to restrict immigration so that we may continue to receive its benefits while at the same time the welfare of the country is safeguarded against its evils, is the issue. . . .

It is a curious fact, but none the less a fact, that too much, even of something that in moderate amounts is good for us, may become very injurious—so injurious as to necessitate the regulation of the quantity we should have. The quantity of present immigration is no bugaboo but a real danger threatening most seriously the success of "The American Experiment" in government and social organisation. It is such as to over-tax our wonderful powers of assimilation. . . .

IMMIGRATION SHOULD CEASE

I have become convinced that the safety of our institutions, the continuity of our prosperity, the preservation of our standards of living, and the maintaining of a decent level of morals among us depends upon a most rigid limitation of immigration and the maintaining of a rigid standard as to even those few who may be admitted.

Albert Johnson, *The Alien in Our Midst*, 1930.

In the case of the immigration stream now pouring in huge volume into the United States, have we, through our public schools and like safeguards, erected a sufficiently strong dam to protect our institutions? Our forefathers bequeathed to us an educational system that was designed and which was supposed to be strong enough to withstand any flood of ignorance that might beat against our institutions. But this system was not devised in any of its particulars to care for the great volume of ignorance which is now washing into the United States with tremendous force from out of eastern and southern Europe. In many respects it is even now too late to strengthen this educational system. What effect is this volume of ignorance, which is breaking in and overflowing our safeguards, to have on political and religious structures and our social and national life? . . .

The American Republic, with its valuable institutions, approaches the parting of the ways. Fortunately the writing on the signboards is plain. The choice the people are to make as to which way they shall go will determine the kind of civilisation that is to have its home in the United States for coming generations. This choice has to be made—there is no way out of it. It will be made even if no political or governmental action is taken. In this case the choice will be to continue our present policy of unrestricted immigration in cheap labour. This will mean a continuance of the development in feverish haste of the country's material resources by an inpouring of labourers with low standards of living and the perpetuation of a debased citizenship among both the exploited and the exploiters.

The alternative is to restrict immigration so that we can catch our breath and take an inventory of what we already have among us that must imperatively be raised to a higher standard of living and a safer citizenship.

AMERICA'S CHOICE

Our decision means a choice between two conditions. By continuing our present policy we choose that which is producing a plutocratic caste class of idle nobodies resting upon the industrial slavery of a great mass of ignorant and low standard of living toilers. By restricting immigration we influence the bringing about of a condition that will give to a large body of citizens a decent and comfortable standard of living. This desired result is to be obtained by a more just distribution of wealth through wages and prices and dividends.

| "Immigration to the United States
suffers from too much legislation."

RESTRICTIONS ON IMMIGRATION ARE NOT NECESSARY (1912)

Peter Roberts

Peter Roberts (1859–1932) was a Congregationalist pastor and the author of several books on immigrants. The following viewpoint is excerpted from *The New Immigration*, a study of immigrants from southern and eastern Europe first published in 1912. Roberts argues that these immigrants have been beneficial to the United States. He maintains that more legislation restricting immigration is unnecessary and calls for Americans to accept these new immigrants.

As you read, consider the following questions:

1. In the author's opinion, how are commonly accepted stereotypes of immigrants incorrect?
2. According to the author, how do immigrants affect jobs and wages?
3. What does the United States suffer from, according to Roberts?

Excerpted from *The New Immigration* by Peter Roberts. New York: Arno Press, 1970.

All students of immigration should try to do two things: first, get the facts, argue from them, and discard popular prejudices and antipathies—we want to know conditions as they are and not as the biased imagine them to be; second, not to lay at the door of the foreigners evils and conditions which are due to the cupidity, short-sightedness, and inefficiency of the native-born.

"The Scum of the Earth"

The statements that the millions of "the distressed and unfortunate of other lands and climes," "the scum of Europe," "the beaten men of beaten races," "the inefficient, impoverished, and diseased," seek American shores, are untrue, uncharitable, and malicious. Emigration from any land, taken as a whole, is made up of the most vigorous, enterprising, and strongest members of the race. No one denies this when the character of the immigrants who came to America in 1820–1880 is discussed. Censors and prophets of evil proclaimed the stereotyped catalogue of calamities when they came, but their fears were not realized; the men made good and their children are an honor to the nation. The men of the new immigration are now under the eye of the censor, and the prophets of calamities are not wanting, but those who know the newer immigrants intimately believe that they, as their predecessors, will make good and that their children will be an honor to us, if the same opportunities are given these men and thirty years of American influences are allowed to shape and mold their lives. In the winning of the West, the Atlantic states lost much of its best blood by migration, and the same may be said of the exodus of young men from southeastern European countries to America. Every European government, losing its workers by emigration, bemoans the fact and is looking around for some means to check the outflow of strong manhood: would any of them do this if the "scum," "the unfortunate," "the beaten" emigrated?. . .

The slums of Europe are not sent here. The facts and figures of immigration to the United States clearly show that the men of the new immigration come from the farm, and they compare favorably in bodily form and strength with men raised in agricultural communities elsewhere. In the stream, undesirables are found, but the percentage is low. Taken as a whole, they do not show moral turpitude above the average of civilized men. Although transplanted into a new environment, living under abnormal conditions in industrial centers, and meeting more temptations in a week than they would in a lifetime in rural communities in the homeland, yet when their criminal record is compared with that of the native-born males, it comes out better than even.

All the immigrants landed do not stay here. In the decade 1900–1910, 8,795,386 arrived, but the last census enumerators only found 13,343,583 foreign-born in the United States, as against 10,213,817, in 1900. These figures clearly indicate that little more than 60 per cent of the total arrivals of that decade were in the country in 1910. A large percentage of this returning stream represents men and women who could not stand the stress and strain of American life; or, in other words, the unfit were more carefully weeded out by industrial competition than by the laws regulating immigration. This again works in favor of virile accretions to the population of the United States.

COMPOSITION OF IMMIGRANTS BY DECADES

	From Northwest Europe	From Southeast Europe	All Others
	Per Cent	Per Cent	Per Cent
1821–1830	76.5	8.0	15.5
1831–1840	84.3	10.0	5.7
1841–1850	93.4	5.1	1.5
1851–1860	93.3	4.3	2.4
1861–1870	85.5	10.9	3.6
1871–1880	72.0	16.5	11.5
1881–1890	68.0	18.9	12.1
1891–1900	48.2	51.0	2.8
1901–1910	26.1	65.9	8.0

Peter Roberts, *The New Immigration*, 1912.

We constantly hear about the stream of gold going to Europe, which reached high-water mark in 1907, the year when immigration exceeded a million and a quarter, and the industrial boom was at its height. In that year, the Immigration Commission estimated the amount of money sent back to Europe at $275,000,000. America is a great country, and this sum should be compared with our industrial and commercial importance. The value of the coal mined that year was nearly two and a half times larger than the sum sent to Europe; the products of our mines were eight times as valuable; our commerce with foreign countries aggregated a sum more than eleven times as great; the value of the produce of the farms of the United States was twenty-one times as great; the value of the products of our manufacturing was fifty times larger; and if we compare the sum sent by immigrants to Europe during this year of prosperity with the total estimated wealth of the nation in 1907, it is about two-tenths of one per cent. Can the economists and statesmen, who, in this great country of ours, become excited over this item, as if the welfare of America depended upon its retention on this side of the water, be taken seriously? We don't think they take themselves seriously. . . .

But we are told that "the immigrants most dangerous are those who come . . . to earn the *higher wages* offered in the United States, with the fixed intention of returning to their families in the home country to spend those wages." The fact is, that the immigrants earn the *lower wages* offered in the United States, suffer most from intermittent and seasonal labor, and, being largely employed in hazardous industries, pay the major part of the loss of life and limb incident to these operations. The country owes a debt to every immigrant who returns having spent many years of his life in our industrial army. . . .

THE STANDARD OF LIVING

We are also told that the foreigners have reduced wages and affected the American standard of living. On the first point, the Department of Commerce and Labor, after long and patient investigation, has failed to find a reduction in wage in the industries largely manned by immigrants.

Is it not a fact that wages were never as high in the industries of the United States as in 1907, the year when immigration touched high-water mark and 1,285,349 came to America? The immigrants from southeastern Europe, when they understand what the standard wage is, will fight for it with far greater solidarity than the Anglo-Saxon or the Teuton. The most stubborn strikes in recent years have been the anthracite coal strike, the McKees Rocks, the Westmoreland, etc., in each of which the men of the new immigration were in the majority. It would be difficult to give concrete instances of foreigners actually reducing wages, but many instances may be given where they have stubbornly resisted a reduction and bravely fought for an increased wage. As to the second point, the American standard of living is a shifting one. In the mill towns and mine patches of West Virginia, North Carolina, and Alabama, the foreigners would have to come down many degrees in order to conform with the standard of living of Americans of purest blood. In a town in New England, a banker said that the New England Yankee was in his capacity to save money a close second to the Magyar, who led the foreigners in this respect. Put the native-born on $450 a year—the average wage of foreigners—and will he be able to build a home, raise a family, and push the children several degrees up in the economic scale? The immigrants are doing this. Suppose the new immigration had kept away, would the wages of unskilled labor be higher? This leads us to the region of conjecture. One thing we know, that the wage has steadily advanced notwithstanding the unprecedented inflow of the last decade. . . .

THE DECLARATION OF INDEPENDENCE

A little attention to the principles involved would have convinced us long ago that an American citizen who preaches wholesale restriction of immigration is guilty of political heresy. The Declaration of Independence accords to *all* men an equal share in the inherent rights of humanity. When we go contrary to that principle, we are not acting as Americans; for, by definition, an American is one who lives by the principles of the Declaration. And we surely violate the Declaration when we attempt to exclude aliens on account of race, nationality, or economic status. "*All* men" means yellow men as well as white men, men from the South of Europe as well as men from the North of Europe, men who hold kingdoms in pawn, and men who owe for their dinner. We shall have to recall officially the Declaration of Independence before we can lawfully limit the application of its principles to this or that group of men.

Mary Antin, *They Who Knock at Our Gates*, 1914.

We are further told that "the immigrants are not *additional* inhabitants," but that "their coming displaces the native stock"; "that the racial suicide is closely connected with the problem of immigration." If "racial suicide" were a phenomenon peculiar to the United States, there would be force in the argument. There is no immigration into France, and yet sterility and a low birth rate have been the concern of statesmen and moralists in that country for the last quarter of a century. The same phenomenon is observed among the middle classes in England and the Scandinavian peninsula. Artificial restriction on natality is practiced in every industrial country by men and women whose income is such that they must choose between raising a family or maintaining their social status. One or the other of these two institutions must suffer and it is generally the family. This is the case in America. The native-born clerk, tradesman, machinist, professional man, etc., whose income ranges between $800 and $1200 a year, can hardly risk matrimony in an urban community. If he does take a wife, they can hardly afford to raise one child, while two cause great anxiety. A low birth rate is a condition that is superinduced by industrial development. The opportunity for advancement, social prestige, love of power and its retention in the family, etc., these are some of the causes of a low birth rate. "But greater than any other cause is 'the deliberate and voluntary avoidance of child-bearing on the part of a steadily increasing number of married people, who not only prefer to have but few children, but who know how to obtain their wish,'" [according to W.B. Bailey]. Immigration is no more the cause of racial suicide than the countryside superstition that a plentiful crop of nuts is the cause of fecundity. . . .

IMMIGRANTS DO NEEDED WORK

The foreigners are despised for the work they do. Must this work be done? Can America get along without sewer digging, construction work, tunnel driving, coal mining, meat packing, hide tanning, etc.—disagreeable work, which the English-speaking shun? This labor is necessary and the foreigners do it uncomplainingly. Should they be condemned, despised, and dubbed "the scum of the earth" for doing basic work which we all know is a necessity, but which we ourselves will not perform? A percentage of foreigners is illiterate, and a still larger percentage is unskilled, but every one who has studied these men knows that they have common sense, meekness, patience submission, docility, and gratitude—qualities which have made them admirably suited for the coarse work America needs done. The accident of birth accounts largely for skill in reading and writing as well as for a knowledge of the trades: we cannot choose the country of our birth any more than hereditary tendencies; why, then, should we blame men for the consequence of these accidents? The best judges of America's need of unskilled labor are employers, men of affairs, and leaders in the industrial development of the nation, and these without exception say that the foreigner has been a blessing and not a curse. In 1910, the National Board of Trade received letters from ninety-three such men, residing in thirty-five states, expressing their views as to the effect of immigration on labor and the industries, and the following is the summary of their answers:—

1. That the general effect of immigration to this country has been beneficial.

2. That immigration so far has not constituted a menace to American labor.

3. That it is still needed for our industrial and commercial development.

In view of these conclusions, the right of the foreigner to respect and honorable treatment from Americans ought to be acknowledged; the credit due him for the part he has played in the industrial development of America should be freely given; his right to the free enjoyment of the fruit of his labor wherever he chooses to spend his money should be conceded; but unfortunately none of these rights is recognized by a vast number of native-born men in the immigration zone. . . .

IMMIGRANTS AND PROSPERITY

The economic supremacy of the United States was attained during the very period when large numbers of immigrants were coming into the country. . . .

Immigrants have contributed greatly to the industrial development of this country; contributed not alone by their numbers but also by their age, sex and training.

Constantine Panunzio, *Immigration Crossroads*, 1927.

We have reason to believe that immigration to the United States suffers from too much legislation. Multiplicity of laws will not secure to the United States immunity from the evils of immigration. Each new barrier erected invites the cunning and duplicity of shrewd foreigners to overcome it and affords an opportunity to exploit the ignorant. It is the duty of the government to guard the gates against the diseased, the insane, and the criminal, and our present laws, in the hands of competent men, do this. The immigrant has a right to look for transportation conveniences on steamships and accommodations in detention stations, which comply with the demands of sanitary science and personal hygiene. Every important distributing center should have detention halls, where the immigrants could be kept until called for by friends or guided by responsible parties to their destination. America collects $4 per head from all immigrants coming to the country. Canada spends that amount per head to give the newcomers the necessary information as to agricultural opportunities and economic conditions, so that the men may exercise their judgement as to place to locate and employment to seek. The immigrants will never be distributed in the states and the communities where their labor would count for most, as long as the hands of the division of information of the Bureau of Immigration are tied by the want of funds to fulfill the purpose for which it was created. The attempt to regulate the inflow of immigrants by legislation according to the labor supply of this country is impracticable and will inevitably lead to political skirmishing. Who is to decide the condition of the labor market, the operators or the trades-union? Economic law will regulate this far more effectually and promptly. While the recommendations of the Immigration Commission wait the action of Congress, industrial depression has driven 2,000,000 workers out of the country. If the "Conclusions and Recommendations" of the Commission were written in 1907 instead of 1910, their tone would be very different. A few efficient laws left alone and well executed are better than many statutes, continuous legislative tinkering, and inefficiency.

The assimilation of the immigrants must depend more upon private effort than upon legislation. No action of either Federal or state government can do half as much for aliens wishing to join the family as the conduct of Americans in the immigration zone, who can help this cause more by throwing open the school building than by urging the enactment of state laws concerning the illiteracy of foreigners. Centers opened in every public school in foreign colonies, where immigrants could be taught, would do more for foreigners in one year, than ten years of legislative inhibition as to what the foreigners should or should not do. . . .

Legislative action and private organizations can do much for immigrants, but the most effective of all remedies is personal contact. We can legislate as we have a mind to, but unless the native-born is ready to take the foreign-born in confidence and sympathy into the family, there will be no assimilation. Of the 13,500,000 foreign-born in the country at present, about half of them are from southeastern Europe: in other words in a population of 90,000,000 whites, just one out of every fifteen is a child of the backward races of Europe, and we all stand in awe of him and say he is a menace. Would it not be better to trust the brother, believe that he is capable of infinite good, give him a fair chance in the race, secure to him all freedom of opportunity, and treat him at all times as a responsible moral being with rights and duties as other men? If this personal touch is secured, righteous treatment given, and broad sympathetic interest shown, the immigration problem will be solved in the light of the brotherhood of man and the spirit of our democracy.

"The use of a national origins system is without basis in either logic or reason."

NATIONAL ORIGINS QUOTAS SHOULD BE ABOLISHED (1963)

John F. Kennedy

In 1921 and 1924, Congress passed laws that placed limits on immigration. These laws awarded each foreign country immigration quotas based on the ethnic composition of the United States. The effect of the laws, revised but not significantly changed in 1952, was to sharply limit immigration from southern and eastern Europe, as well as Africa and Asia. Many people criticized this quota system as being racist and at odds with American values. In the following viewpoint, John F. Kennedy (1917–1963) argues that this system of national origins quotas is embarrassing to the United States and should be eliminated. Kennedy, a great-grandson of Irish immigrants, was elected president of the United States in 1960. Many of the ideas Kennedy states in this viewpoint were enacted into law in 1965, two years after he was assassinated.

As you read, consider the following questions:

1. What were the motivations behind the immigration laws of 1921 and 1924, according to Kennedy?
2. Why are national origins quotas racist, according to the author?
3. What reforms to U.S. immigration law does Kennedy propose?

From the start, immigration policy has been a prominent subject of discussion in America. This is as it must be in a democracy, where every issue should be freely considered and debated.

AMBIGUOUS ATTITUDES

Immigration, or rather the British policy of clamping down on immigration, was one of the factors behind the colonial desire for independence. Restrictive immigration policies constituted one of the charges against King George III expressed in the Declaration of Independence. And in the Constitutional Convention James Madison noted, "That part of America which has encouraged them [the immigrants] has advanced most rapidly in population, agriculture and the arts." So, too, Washington in his Thanksgiving Day Proclamation of 1795 asked all Americans "humbly and fervently to beseech the kind Author of these blessings . . . to render this country more and more a safe and propitious asylum for the unfortunate of other countries."

Yet there was the basic ambiguity which older Americans have often shown toward newcomers. In 1797 a member of Congress argued that, while a liberal immigration policy was fine when the country was new and unsettled, now that America had reached its maturity and was fully populated, immigration should stop—an argument which has been repeated at regular intervals throughout American history. . . .

By the turn of the century the opinion was becoming widespread that the numbers of new immigrants should be limited. Those who were opposed to all immigration and all "foreigners" were now joined by those who believed sincerely, and with some basis in fact, that America's capacity to absorb immigration was limited. This movement toward restricting immigration represented a social and economic reaction, not only to the tremendous increase in immigration after 1880, but also to the shift in its main sources, to Southern, Eastern and Southeastern Europe.

THE QUOTA SYSTEM

Anti-immigration sentiment was heightened by World War I, and the disillusionment and strong wave of isolationism that marked its aftermath. It was in this climate, in 1921, that Congress passed and the President signed the first major law in our country's history severely limiting new immigration by establishing an emergency quota system. An era in American history had ended, we were committed to a radically new policy toward the peopling of the nation.

The Act of 1921 was an early version of the so-called "national origins" system. Its provisions limited immigration of numbers of each nationality to a certain percentage of the number of foreign-born individuals of that nationality resident in the United States according to the 1910 census. Nationality meant country of birth. The total number of immigrants permitted to enter under this system each year was 357,000.

In 1924 the Act was revised, creating a temporary arrangement for the years 1924 to 1929, under which the national quotas for 1924 were equal to 2 percent of the number of foreign-born persons of a given nationality living in the United States in 1890, or about 164,000 people. The permanent system, which went into force in 1929, includes essentially all the elements of immigration policy that are in our law today. The immigration statutes now establish a system of annual quotas to govern immigration from each country. Under this system 156,987 quota immigrants are permitted to enter the United States each year. The quotas from each country are based upon the national origins of the population of the United States in 1920.

The use of the year 1920 is arbitrary. It rests upon the fact that this system was introduced in 1924 and the last prior census was in 1920. The use of a national origins system is without basis in either logic or reason. It neither satisfies a national need nor accomplishes an international purpose. In an age of interdependence among nations such a system is an anachronism, for it discriminates among applicants for admission into the United States on the basis of accident of birth.

THE SYSTEM FAVORS NORTHERN EUROPE

Because of the composition of our population in 1920, the system is heavily weighted in favor of immigration from Northern Europe and severely limits immigration from Southern and Eastern Europe and from other parts of the world.

To cite some examples: Great Britain has an annual quota of 65,361 immigration visas and used 28,291 of them. Germany has a quota of 25,814 and used 26,533 (of this number, about one third are wives of servicemen who could enter on a non-quota basis). Ireland's quota is 17,756 and only 6,054 Irish availed themselves of it. On the other hand, Poland is permitted 6,488, and there is a backlog of 61,293 Poles wishing to enter the United States. Italy is permitted 5,666 and has a backlog of 132,435. Greece's quota is 308; her backlog is 96,538. Thus a Greek citizen desiring to emigrate to this country has little chance of coming here. And an American citizen with a Greek father or mother must wait at least eighteen months to bring his parents here to join him. A citizen whose married son or daughter, or brother or sister, is Italian cannot obtain a quota number for them for two years or more. Meanwhile, many thousands of quota numbers are wasted because they are not wanted or needed by nationals of the countries to which they are assigned.

"What Happened To The One We Used To Have?"

Source: From *The Herblock Book* (Beacon Press, 1952). Reprinted with permission.

In short, a qualified person born in England or Ireland who wants to emigrate to the United States can do so at any time. A person born in Italy, Hungary, Poland or the Baltic States may have to wait many years before his turn is reached. This system is based upon the assumption that there is some reason for keeping the origins of our population in exactly the same proportions as they existed in 1920. Such an idea is at complete variance with the American traditions and principles that the qualification of an immigrant do not depend upon his country of birth, and violates the spirit expressed in the Declaration of Independence that "all men are created equal."

One writer has listed six motives behind the Act of 1924. They were: (1) postwar isolationism; (2) the doctrine of the alleged superiority of Anglo-Saxon and Teutonic "races"; (3) the fear that "pauper labor" would lower wage levels; (4) the belief that people of certain nations were less law-abiding than others; (5) the fear of foreign ideologies and subversion; (6) the fear that entrance of too many people with different customs and habits would undermine our national and social unity and order. All of these arguments can be found in Congressional debates on the subject and may be heard today in discussions over a new national policy toward immigration. Thus far, they have prevailed. The policy of 1924 was continued in all its essentials by the Immigration and Nationality Act of 1952. . . .

1952 REVISIONS

The Immigration and Nationality Act of 1952 undertook to codify all our national laws on immigration. This was a proper and long overdue task. But it was not just [a] housekeeping chore. In the course of the deliberation over the Act, many basic decisions about our immigration policy were made. The total racial bar against the naturalization of Japanese, Koreans and other East Asians was removed, and a minimum annual quota of one hundred was provided for each of these countries. Provision was also made to make it easier to reunite husbands and wives. Most important of all was the decision to do nothing about the national origins system.

The famous words of Emma Lazarus on the pedestal of the Statue of Liberty read: "Give me your tired, your poor, your huddled masses yearning to breathe free." Until 1921 this was an accurate picture of our society. Under present law it would be appropriate to add: "as long as they come from Northern Europe, are not too tired or too poor or slightly ill, never stole a loaf of bread, never joined any questionable organization, and can document their activities for the past two years."

INDEFENSIBLE RACIAL PREFERENCE

Furthermore, the national origins quota system has strong overtones of an indefensible racial preference. It is strongly weighted toward so-called Anglo-Saxons, a phrase which one writer calls "a term of art" encompassing almost anyone from Northern and Western Europe. Sinclair Lewis described his hero, Martin Arrowsmith, this way: "a typical pure-bred-Anglo-Saxon American—which means that he was a union of German, French, Scotch-Irish, perhaps a little Spanish, conceivably of the strains lumped together as 'Jewish,' and a great deal of English, which is itself a combination of primitive Britain, Celt, Phoenician, Roman, German, Dane and Swede."

Yet, however much our present policy may be deplored, it still remains our national policy. As President Truman said when he vetoed the Immigration and Nationality Act (only to have that veto overridden): "The idea behind this discriminatory policy was, to put it boldly, that Americans with English or Irish names were better people and better citizens than Americans with Italian or Greek or Polish names. . . . Such a concept is utterly unworthy of our traditions and our ideals.". . .

IMMIGRANTS' CONTRIBUTIONS

One can go on and on pointing out the contributions made by immigrants to our arts, economic growth, health, and culture in general. . . . We should continue by all means to receive these people and facilitate their entry into the United States by doing away with the inequities of the national origins quota system.

America is based upon equality and fair play but our present immigration laws are contrary to the basic principles of this democracy.

A change in our immigration laws is long overdue.

John Papandreas, testimony before Congress, August 7, 1964.

There is, of course, a legitimate argument for some limitation upon immigration. We no longer need settlers for virgin lands, and our economy is expanding more slowly than in the nineteenth and early twentieth centuries. . . .

The clash of opinion arises not over the number of immigrants to be admitted, but over the test for admission—the national origins quota system. Instead of using the discriminatory test of where the immigrant was born, the reform proposals would base admission on the immigrant's possession of skills our country needs and on the humanitarian ground of reuniting families. Such legislation does not seek to make over the face of America. Immigrants would still be given tests for health, intelligence, morality and security. . . .

Religious and civic organizations, ethnic associations and newspaper editorials, citizens from every walk of life and groups of every description have expressed their support for a more rational and less prejudiced immigration law. Congressional leaders of both parties have urged the adoption of new legislation that would eliminate the most objectionable features of the [1952] McCarran-Walter Act and the nationalities quota system. . . .

A FORMULA FOR IMMIGRATION

The Presidential message to Congress of July 23, 1963, recommended that the national origins system be replaced by a formula governing immigration to the United States which takes into account: (1) the skills of the immigrant and their relationships to our needs; (2) the family relationship between immigrants and persons already here, so that the reuniting of families is encouraged; and (3) the priority of registration. Present law grants a preference to immigrants with special skills, education or training. It also grants a preference to various relatives of the United States' citizens and lawfully resident aliens. But it does so only within a national origins quota. It should be modified so that those with the greatest ability to add to the national welfare, no matter where they are born, are granted the highest priority. The next priority should go to those who seek to be reunited with their relatives. For applicants with equal claims, the earliest registrant should be the first admitted. . . .

These changes will not solve all the problems of immigration. But they will insure that progress will continue to be made toward our ideals and toward the realization of humanitarian objectives.

We must avoid what the Irish poet John Boyle O'Reilly once called

Organized charity, scrimped and iced,
In the name of a cautious, statistical Christ.

Immigration policy should be generous; it should be fair; it should be flexible. With such a policy we can turn to the world, and to our own past, with clean hands and a clear conscience. Such a policy would be but a reaffirmation of old principles. It would be an expression of our agreement with George Washington that "The bosom of America is open to receive not only the opulent and respectable stranger, but the oppressed and persecuted of all nations and religions; whom we shall welcome to a participation of all our rights and privileges, if by decency and propriety of conduct they appear to merit the enjoyment."

> "Without the quota system, it is doubtful whether or not America could indefinitely maintain its traditional heritage."

NATIONAL ORIGINS QUOTAS SHOULD BE RETAINED (1964)

Marion Moncure Duncan

Marion Moncure Duncan (1912–1978) was president general of the Daughters of the American Revolution from 1962 to 1965. DAR is a patriotic and social organization composed of female descendants of Revolutionary War veterans. The following viewpoint is taken from Duncan's 1964 testimony before Congress in which she argues against revising immigration law. Duncan asserts that national origins quotas, which since 1921 had limited immigration from places other than northern Europe, should be retained in order to maintain ethnic unity in the United States.

As you read, consider the following questions:

1. What should be the goals of immigration law, according to Duncan?
2. How are contemporary immigrants different from past immigrants, according to the author?
3. In Duncan's opinion, why are national origins quotas necessary?

Marion Moncure Duncan, statement before the U.S. House of Representatives Committee on the Judiciary, August 10, 1964.

I speak in support of maintaining the existing provisions of the Immigration and Nationality Act of 1952, especially the national origins quota system. . . .

I speak not as a specialist or authority in a particular field. Rather, the focus is that of attempting to present to you and ask your consideration of the conscientious convictions of an organization keenly and, more importantly, actively interested in this subject almost since its own inception nearly three-quarters of a century ago. . . .

The DAR is not taking a stand against immigration per se. Any inference in that direction is in error and completely false. DAR, as a national organization, is among the foremost "to extend a helping hand" to immigrants admitted on an intelligent, orderly, equitable basis such as is allowed under the current Immigration and Nationality Act of 1952. If, from time to time, there be need for change or adjustment, it should be provided through logical, deliberate amendment, still retaining the national origins quota system and other vitally basic, protective features of the law. These constitute a first line of defense in perpetuating and maintaining our institutions of freedom and the American way of life. To discard them would endanger both.

From the point that immigration is definitely a matter of national welfare and security, it is imperative that a logical and rational method of governing and administering same be maintained. The [1952] Walter-McCarran Act has done and will continue equitably to accomplish just this. It denies no nation a quota, but it does provide a reasonable, orderly, mathematical formula (based, of course, upon the 1920 census figures) which is devoid of the political pressure which could inevitably be expected to beset any commission authorized to reapportion unused quotas as proposed in the legislation before you.

THE 1952 IMMIGRATION ACT

By way of background: What prompted passage of the Immigration-Nationality Act of 1952? It will be recalled that this was the product of a tedious, comprehensive study of nearly 5 years' duration, covering some 200 laws on selective immigration, special orders and exclusions, and spanned the period from passage of the first quota law by Congress in 1924. This law codified and coordinated all existing immigration, nationality, and deportation laws.

Despite repeated efforts to weaken, circumvent and bypass this protective legislation, its soundness has been demonstrated over the period it has been in operation.

It embodies the following important features—all in the best interest of our constitutional republic:

(a) Recognizing the cultural identity and historic population basis of this Nation, it officially preserved the national origin quota system as the basis for immigration, wisely giving preference to those nations whose composite culture—Anglo-Saxon from northern and western European countries—has been responsible for and actually produced the American heritage as we know it today.

(b) It abolished certain discriminatory provisions in our immigration laws—those against sexes and persons of Asiatic origin.

(c) "Quality versus quantity" preference for skilled aliens was provided, as well as broadened classifications for nonquota immigrants. No nation or race is listed ineligible for immigration and naturalization, although the acknowledged purpose is to preserve this country's culture, free institutions, free enterprise economy and racial complex, yes, and likely even language. Ready assimilability of the majority of immigrants is a prime factor.

(d) It provides the U.S. Immigration Department with needed authority to cope with subversive aliens by strengthening security provisions.

THE UNITED STATES MUST BE SELECTIVE

We will gain neither respect, gratitude, nor love from other nations by making our homes their doormat. Nations, like men, must be reasonably selective about whom they adopt into the bosom of their family. . . .

We cannot maintain our priceless heritage of individual liberty as outlined in the three classic cornerstones of our Republic; in the Declaration of Independence, our Federal and State Constitutions, and our Bill of Rights, if we permit our already overpacked "melting pot," to be inundated from the world's most deprived areas; or if we break down those barriers which now permit us to screen out those who neither know, nor appreciate, the value of American institutions or the aims of our great country.

Myra C. Hacker, statement before Congress, August 11, 1964.

Perhaps the sentiment and deep concern of the DAR relative to the matter of immigration and its appeal for retention of the present law is best expressed by excerpting salient points from recent resolutions on the subject:

(1) For building unity and cohesiveness among American citizens, whose social, economic and spiritual mind has been and

is under increasing pressures and conflicts, wise and comprehensive steps must be taken.

(2) For the protection and interest of all citizens from foreign elements imbued with ideologies wholly at variance with our republican form of government should be excluded.

On basis of FBI [Federal Bureau of Investigation] analysis statistics and information available through investigation by the House Un-American Activities Committee, loopholes through which thousands of criminal aliens may enter this country constitute a continuing threat for the safety of American institutions.

(3) Since it is a recognized fact that free migration allowing unhampered movement of agents is necessary for triumph of either a world socialist state or international communism as a world conspiracy, this would explain the motivation on the part of enemies of this country for concentrated effort to undermine the existing immigration law.

(4) Admittedly, major problems confronting the Nation and threatening its national economy are unemployment, housing, education, security, population explosion, and other domestic problems such as juvenile delinquency, crime, and racial tensions. This is borne out by numerous statistics and the current Federal war on poverty effort. In view of this, revisions as per proposed new quotas to greatly increase the number of immigrants would be a threat to the security and well-being of this Nation, especially in face of the cold war inasmuch as it would be impossible to obtain adequate security checks on immigrants from satellite Communist-controlled countries.

In summation: A comparative study would indicate increased aggravation of existing problems and unfavorable repercussions on all facets of our economy such as employment, housing, education, welfare, health, and national security, offering additional threats to the American heritage—cultural, social, and ethnic traditions. . . .

THE DIFFERENCE BETWEEN THEN AND NOW

While DAR would be the first to admit the importance of immigrants to America, its membership ties linking directly with the first waves of immigrants to these shores, it would seem well, however, to point out a "then and now" difference factor currently exists attributable to time and circumstance—no uncomplimentary inference therein. A common desire shared by immigrants of all time to America has been the seeking of freedom or the escape from tyranny. But in the early days, say the first 150 years, it is noteworthy that those who came shared common

Anglo-Saxon bonds and arrived with the full knowledge and intent of founders or pioneers who knew there was a wilderness to conquer and a nation to build. Their coming indicated a willingness to make a contribution and assume such a role. In the intervening years, many fine, high-caliber immigrants, and I know some at personal sacrifice, following ideals in which they believed, have likewise come to America imbued with a constructive desire to produce and add to the glory of their new homeland. They, however, have come to a nation already established with cultural patterns set and traditions already rooted.

Further, in recent years, en masse refugee movements, though responding to the very same ideal which is America, have been motivated primarily by escape. This has had a tendency possibly to dim individual purpose and dedication and possibly project beyond other considerations, the available benefits to be secured as an American citizen.

The Quota System Is Fair

The fact is that the national origins quota system does not predicate the quotas upon the race, culture, morality, intelligence, health, physical attributes, or any other characteristics of the people in any foreign country.

The quotas are based upon our own people. The national origins system is like a mirror held up before the American people and reflecting the proportions of their various foreign national origins.

Assertions by critics that the national origins system is in some way discriminatory or establishes the principle that some foreign nations or ethnic groups are defined as "superior" or "inferior" are entirely without foundation.

National origins simply attempts to have immigration into the United States conform in composition to our own people.

John B. Trevor Jr., testimony before Congress, May 20, 1965.

Abandonment of the national origins system would drastically alter the source of our immigration. Any change would not take into consideration that those whose background and heritage most closely resemble our own are most readily assimilable.

In testimony before you, this point was touched upon by a high official when he said, "To apply the new principle rigidly would result, after a few years, in eliminating immigration from these countries almost entirely." Admittedly such a situation would be undesirable. A strict first-come, first-served basis of allocating visa quotas as proposed would create certain problems in countries of northern and western Europe, and could ultimately dry up influx from that area.

Going a step further, would not the abolishment of the national origin quota system work a hardship and possibly result in actual discrimination against the very nations who supplied the people who now comprises the majority of our historic population mixture? Further, such a change in our existing laws would appear to be an outright accommodation to the heaviest population explosions throughout the world—India, Asia, and Africa. Certainly these countries could naturally be expected to take full advantage of such an increased quota opportunity.

Is it, therefore, desirable or in the best interest to assign possible 10-percent quotas to say proliferating African nations to the end that our own internal problems become manifold? America, as all other nations, is concerned over rapid population growth of this era. Staggering statistics are readily available on every hand.

IMMIGRATION IS A PRIVILEGE

Attention is called to the fact that immigration is not an alien's right; it is a privilege. With privilege comes its handmaiden responsibility. Before tampering with the present immigration law, much less destroying its basic principles, due regard must also be given to our own unemployment situation. No less an authority than the late President John F. Kennedy, who was for this bill, stated on March 3, 1963, that we had 5 million unemployed and 2 million people displaced each year by advancing technology and automation.

Irrespective of recent and reoccurring reports on unemployment showing temporary increases or decreases, the fact is, it remains a matter of economic concern. Latest figures available as of June 1964 indicate 4.7 million or 5.3 percent.

In view of this, it would seem highly incongruent if not outright incredible to find ourselves in a situation, on the one hand, waging war on poverty and unemployment at home, while on the other hand, simultaneously and indiscriminately letting down immigration bars to those abroad. Not only employment alone but mental health and retardation problems could greatly increase. Another source of concern to the heavy laden taxpayer to whom already the national debt figure is astronomical.

It is asserted that our economy will get three consumers for every worker admitted and that our economy generates jobs at a rate better than one for every three consumers. Why, then, are we presently plagued with unemployment? And how is it possible to guarantee that these new immigrants will "fill jobs that are going begging because there are not enough skilled workers in our economy who have the needed skills?" Are there enough such jobs going begging to justify destroying an immigration law which has been described as our first line of defense?

Rightly, it would seem U.S. citizens should have first claim on jobs and housing in this country. With manpower available and the recent emphasis on expanded educational facilities, why is not definite concentrated effort made to provide and accelerate vocational and special skill training for the many who either through disinclination, native inability or otherwise are not qualified potentials for schooling in the field of science, medicine, law, or other such professions?

THE NEED FOR NATIONAL QUOTAS

Without the quota system, it is doubtful whether or not America could indefinitely maintain its traditional heritage: Economic, cultural, social, ethnic, or even language.

Free institutions as we have known them would stand to undergo radical change if the proposal to permit reapportionment of unused quotas is also adopted. It is felt reassignment of unused quotas would be as damaging to the basic principles of the Immigration and Nationality Act as repeal of the national origins system itself. . . .

The National Society, Daughters of the American Revolution, which initially supported the Walter-McCarran bill when it was introduced and has continuously done so since, wishes again to officially reaffirm its support of the existing law, firmly believing that the present Immigration and Nationality Act of 1952 not only safeguards our constitutional Republic and perpetuates our American heritage, but by maintaining its established standards, that it actually protects the naturalized American on a par with the native born, and as well offers encouragement to desirable immigrants to become future American citizens. Any breakdown in this system would be an open invitation to Communist infiltration. Likewise, a poor law, newly enacted, and improperly administered, could provide the same opportunity to the detriment, if not the actual downfall, of our country.

The well-intentioned, humanitarian plea that America's unrestricted assumption of the overpopulous, troubled, ailing people of the world within our own borders is unrealistic, impractical, and if done in excess could spell economic bankruptcy for our people from point of both employment and overladen taxes to say nothing of a collapse of morale and spiritual values if nonassimilable aliens of dissimilar ethnic background and culture by wholesale and indiscriminate transporting en masse overturn the balance of our national character.

In connection with the liberalization proposals, it would seem timely to refer to the words of Senator Patrick McCarran, who, when he presented the bill, warned:

> If the enemies of this legislation succeed in riddling it to pieces, or in amending it beyond recognition, they will have contributed more to promote this Nation's downfall than any other group since we achieved our independence as a nation.

Somewhat the same sentiment was expressed by Abraham Lincoln, who admonished:

> You cannot strengthen the weak by weakening the strong; and you cannot help men permanently by doing for them what they could and should do for themselves.

Many inspiring words have been written of America. I would conclude with those of the late historian, James Truslow Adams:

> America's greatest contribution to the world has been that of the American dream, the dream of a land where life shall be richer, fuller, and better, with opportunity for every person according to his ability and achievement.

The question is: Can it continue so if, through reckless abandon, the United States becomes mired, causing the country to lose its image as the land of opportunity, the home of the free? Ours is the responsibility to maintain and preserve it for the future.

IS IMMIGRATION A PROBLEM FOR THE UNITED STATES?

CHAPTER PREFACE

The United States was founded by immigrants, but nearly 400 years later, Americans cannot agree on whether their nation should continue to accept them. According to the Immigration and Naturalization Service (INS), nearly 61 million legal immigrants have come to the United States since 1820, when the first records were kept. The number of legal immigrants has increased dramatically in the last half of the twentieth century. Between 1961 and 1970, 3.3 million legal immigrants entered the United States. That number more than doubled between 1981 and 1990, when 7.3 million legal immigrants came. During the early 1990s, approximately 800,000 legal immigrants and an estimated 300,000 illegal immigrants entered the United States each year.

Critics of U.S. immigration policy argue that the country cannot absorb so many new residents. They contend that the new immigrants lower prevailing wages and take jobs away from Americans. Opponents charge that immigration especially harms America's minorities, many of whom are forced to work for half their former pay if they want to keep their jobs. Lastly, critics assert, taxes paid by immigrants do not cover the costs of the social services, such as welfare, that they receive, nor the education provided for their children.

Supporters of immigration assert, however, that opponents exaggerate or even invent many of the problems attributed to immigration. Immigrants are a necessary part of the workforce, especially in fruit and vegetable harvesting or slaughterhouse work. Many employers prefer immigrant workers because of their strong work ethic and determination to succeed. Furthermore, rather than detracting from the economy, some evidence suggests immigrants enhance it. According to a 1996 report by Harvard economist George Borjas, immigrants add an estimated $7 billion a year to the country's gross national product.

The vision of America as the land of opportunity will continue to encourage people from around the world to come to the United States, either legally or illegally. The authors in the following chapter examine whether these newcomers are more of a boon or burden to their new homeland.

"More than 800,000 legal immigrants . . . every year . . . need jobs . . . and many other services that cannot even be provided to millions of native-born Americans."

LEGAL IMMIGRATION IS A SERIOUS PROBLEM

Yeh Ling-Ling

Mass immigration has a negative effect on the nation's economy and environment, argues Yeh Ling-Ling in the following viewpoint. Mechanization and downsizing have decreased the number of jobs available, she maintains, and the stiff competition for the remaining jobs has therefore lowered wages. Furthermore, Yeh asserts, immigrants' taxes do not cover the costs of providing them with welfare, education, and health care. An immediate five-year moratorium on immigration would save the country money while giving policymakers time to develop an immigration policy. Yeh is the founder of the Diversity Coalition for an Immigration Moratorium in San Francisco.

As you read, consider the following questions:

1. By what percentage did the number of elderly immigrants on welfare increase from 1982 to 1994, according to the author?
2. In Yeh's opinion, what is inaccurate about studies that claim mass immigration is a benefit to the United States?
3. How much does immigration cost the United States in job loss and wage depression, according to George Borjas as cited by the author?

Reprinted from "Legal Immigration Must Be Curbed, Too," by Yeh Ling-Ling, USA Today magazine, January 1997, by permission of the Society for the Advancement of Education.

Year after year, presidential candidates and members of Congress from both parties repeatedly have promised to reduce budget deficits, strengthen the economy, create jobs for Americans, and put welfare recipients back to work. Yet, how can those goals possibly be achieved if the U.S. continues to allow an average of more than 800,000 legal immigrants to enter the country every year? These newcomers need jobs, education, welfare, health care, and many other services that cannot even be provided to millions of native-born Americans.

As a naturalized citizen of Chinese ancestry with extensive professional experience preparing family- and employment-based immigrant petitions, I am disappointed over the lack of will in Washington to reduce legal immigration. This hesitancy continues despite the fact that even strong immigration rights advocates have admitted the adverse impact of mass immigration.

AN ADVERSE IMPACT

Antonia Hernandez, president of the Mexican American Legal Defense and Educational Fund, has stated that "migration, legal and undocumented, does have an impact on our economy. . . . Most of the competition is to the Latino community. We compete with each other for those low-paying jobs. There is an issue of wage depression, as in the garment industry, which is predominantly immigrant. . . ."

Chinese-American Prof. Paul Ong of UCLA, a strong advocate of a liberal immigration policy, points out that "In terms of adverse impact [of immigration] on wages and employment, the adverse impact will be most pronounced on minorities and established immigrants. . . ."

Po Wong, director of the Chinese Newcomers Service Center in San Francisco, indicated in 1993 that, of the 11,000 new Chinese immigrants looking for work through his agency, just 2% were placed successfully. "I don't think our community is equipped to welcome this large a number. . . . It's very depressing to see so many people come here looking for work."

Dolores Huerta, co-founder of the United Farm Workers Union, testified before the California Select Committee on Immigration that "With 1,500,000 legalized immigrants living in California, and only approximately 250,000 agricultural jobs in the state, there is no need for additional farm workers."

The pro-immigration Urban Institute has acknowledged that "less-skilled black workers and black workers in high immigration areas with stagnant economies are negatively affected [by immigration]."

Stanford University law professor Bill Ong Hing, author of a report on contributions of Asian immigrants, cites "a certain legitimacy to the view that parts of the country are being overcrowded with immigrants. . . . They affect growth, air pollution, water availability. It's not bogus for people to raise that issue."

FEWER WORKERS ARE NEEDED

The nation's leaders should be reminded that today's economy requires fewer and fewer workers due to automation, advances in technology, and corporate downsizing. Moreover, many jobs have been lost to foreign countries. If the Federal government continues to allow hundreds of thousands of low-skilled legal immigrants of working age to enter the U.S. every year, how can America's unemployed, low-skilled workers and welfare recipients be expected to find work? Rosy unemployment rates released by the Labor Department do not include millions of workers who are underemployed or never have found work.

U.S. immigration laws have a devastating impact on American professionals as well. In addition to 130,000 employment-based immigrant visas for foreign-born professionals being provided annually, virtually unlimited numbers of various types of "temporary workers" are permitted to enter to work in professional occupations for several years. "H1B [extraordinary ability] temporary workers" alone are estimated to be around 400,000 in this country at any time.

Today's global economy requires highly skilled workers to prosper. If the U.S. does not have sufficient resources to prepare its children and existing legal immigrants to be tomorrow's productive workers, why should the nation invite hundreds of thousands of legal immigrant children to America's already overcrowded schools every year? Fiscally responsible politicians should bear in mind that the cost of educating a child in the U.S. runs about $5,000 a year. If an immigrant child needs an average of eight years of education, it will cost taxpayers $40,000.

In 1994, 740,000 elderly legal immigrants were on welfare, a 580% increase over 1982. (This number did not include the seniors who became naturalized citizens.) Bekki Mar, an immigration advocate working for Self-Help for the Elderly in San Francisco, indicated that 85% of the immigrant clients of her center were on welfare. If a senior immigrant receives welfare, Medicaid, food stamps, and government-subsidized low-income housing, he or she will cost taxpayers a minimum of $100,000 over a five-year period.

More than half of recent legal immigrants are low-skilled and therefore unlikely to pay enough taxes to cover the cost of educating their children. While many immigrants own businesses, they very rarely hire U.S.-born workers. The jobs they create usually are low-paying ones. These low-paying jobs frequently do not generate sufficient tax dollars to cover the cost of all the services rendered to the families of the immigrant employees and employers.

THE COSTS OF IMMIGRATION

Pro-immigration libertarians argue that immigrants help stimulate the economy and create jobs by their consumerism. While immigrant students and welfare recipients are consumers, they require more teachers, classrooms, welfare, and health care. Who is paying the bills if not U.S. taxpayers? George Borjas, a Cuban immigrant and an economics professor at Harvard University, estimates that, in California, 40% of welfare benefits, cash and non-cash, go to immigrants.

Donald Huddle of Rice University projects that the net costs of legal immigration over the next 10 years will exceed $400 billion unless the numbers are reduced drastically. Studies claiming mass immigration to be an economic asset have not computed the cost of all services rendered to immigrants. Moreover, children born in the U.S. of immigrants are left out in their fiscal analyses. Can the U.S. ever balance its budgets without first addressing legal immigration? What price tag should be appended to the daily frustration of dealing with traffic congestion? How can one compute the loss to the U.S. of having a growing semi-illiterate workforce?

Proponents of mass immigration often claim that the nation's computer industry depends on immigration for its technological edge. However, reports on 60 Minutes, 48 Hours, and CNN Presents have shown that American computer professionals have been replaced with foreign-born workers because of companies' desire for a cheaper workforce. Sun Microsystems, a prominent company in California's Silicon Valley lobbying heavily for large-scale immigration, has boasted publicly that it has hired 50 Russian programmers at "bargain prices." Hewlett-Packard also has admitted under oath in court that their engineers from India are of lower quality.

Norman Matloff, former chairman of the Affirmative Action Committee at the University of California, Davis, points out that, out of 56 awards for advances in hardware and software by the Association for Computing Machinery, the nation's main computer science professional society, only one recipient has been an immigrant. Similarly, out of 115 awards given by the Institute of Electrical and Electronics Engineering, just nine recipients have been immigrants.

The large numbers of immigrants in American graduate schools often are cited by advocates to support their claim that immigration continues to be vital to the U.S. economy. Yet, this country has an oversupply of Ph.D.s, as has been reported in many publications and a joint study by Stanford University and RAND Corp.

No Need for Immigration

Today we are letting in over 1 million immigrants legally and around 300,000 illegally. Traditionally, we let in about 200,000 immigrants a year. If we'd admitted immigrants for 200 years at the rate we've admitted them for the past five there would be 2 billion people living in this country today.

In the 1980s, we had the largest sustained wave in American history—around 9 million immigrants entered legally; we gave amnesty to and legalized another 3.1 million aliens in a 1986 act of Congress; and perhaps another 3 million entered illegally in the decade. In the 1990s, those numbers may well go higher still. That makes no sense. We have had far too much immigration in far too few years.

We need to ask basic questions: Are we still trying to fill up an empty continent? Does the United States face an acute labor shortage? We have *no* need for immigration today.

Dan Stein, *American Legion*, April 1995.

Even assuming that immigrants were more talented and productive than Americans, should the U.S. write off its own citizens and invest in those of other nations? If mass immigration is allowed to displace native workers, is it being suggested that unemployed Americans should join the welfare rolls or turn to crime to support their families? Do pro-family leaders realize that extended unemployment can lead to family breakdown?

Cosmetic Change

A token reduction in employment-based visas or requiring employers to pay aliens prevailing wages merely would be a cosmetic change. Politicians truly concerned about protecting American workers at all levels must recognize that expansive family-based immigration, approaching 500,000 annually, and other categories of immigration add hundreds of thousands of immediate and future workers to the labor markets each year. In addition, adjudicators at the U.S. Department of Labor simply do not have the technical knowledge to determine the actual prevailing wages of professional jobs. Furthermore, this country does not have a system to verify that employers actually will pay aliens the wages they claim in their petitions.

A 1995 audit by the Labor Department's Inspector General concluded that "the foreign labor programs . . . do not protect U.S. workers, jobs or wages from foreign labor." The report found that tests imposed on U.S. employers to prove a lack of qualified American workers were "perfunctory at best and a sham at worst."

George Borjas has estimated that immigration costs $133 billion a year in job losses and wage depression to native workers. Addressing corporate downsizing, which mercilessly sheds U.S. workers, without reducing immigration barely would curb corporate greed.

It is true that the U.S. is a nation of immigrants, many of whom have contributed to building this country. However, circumstances have changed drastically. The U.S. now is the greatest debtor nation on Earth. It has an oversupply of labor at all levels. Schools, jails, and freeways are overflowing. America still may have millions of acres of open space, but land area alone cannot support human lives. Millions of prospective immigrants are awaiting opportunities, but there already are 39 million poverty-stricken citizens who are not yet living the American Dream.

SAVING LIMITED RESOURCES

Many people love children, but very few want unlimited numbers of them. Wise and responsible parents want to limit their family sizes so that they can better provide for their existing offspring. Similarly, Washington should curb immigration in order to save limited resources and job opportunities for Americans of all racial backgrounds, as well as legal immigrants already in the U.S.

Reducing legal immigration simply requires an act of Congress signed into law by the President. Illegal immigration can be curbed significantly by taking away the job and benefit magnets in the U.S. through employer sanctions and tamper-proof documents to verify immigration status.

Mass immigration impacts minorities and the working class the most, the very people liberals want to protect. While it is not the cause of all of America's problems, mass immigration does make many of them much more difficult to solve. Because of the scarcity of jobs, mass immigration essentially means a greater demand on the infrastructure and, therefore, government budgets. Those who wish to provide health care and education to citizens of the poor nations should be aware that mass immigration is by no means cost-efficient. The expense of providing those services in developing nations would be a small fraction of what it costs in the U.S.

EXPLOITATION

Liberals opposing immigration reduction must understand that they unintentionally help big businesses, which lobby vigorously for mass immigration, to exploit U.S.-born workers and existing immigrants. Many conservative pro-business politicians favor large-scale immigration because it keeps wages down. They overlook the real and total costs of services rendered to immigrants and their descendants, a burden unduly borne by taxpayers. Welfare legislation passed by Congress in 1996 will continue to give naturalized citizens access to all assistance programs. Aid to legal immigrants is not limited to welfare, Medicaid, food stamps, and government-subsidized low-income housing. The government is required to provide public education from kindergarten to 12th grade; construction and maintenance of roads and bridges; and fire, police, emergency, park, prison, and court services.

Modern transportation and telecommunications can be used to link immigrants with their relatives separated by oceans within hours or minutes. Many countries in the Pacific Rim are experiencing tremendous economic growth. Yet, hundreds of thousands of nationals of those "emerging economies" have been admitted every year to an America that is struggling with economic woes and skyrocketing budget deficits. Meanwhile, many recent Chinese immigrants have Hui Liu (returned to Taiwan, Hong Kong, and China), saying that the U.S. has fewer opportunities than the Far East. They left their children behind for American taxpayers to educate, however!

In 1995, the United Nations recommended that all countries accept a combined total of less than 32,000 refugees. The U.S. alone admitted more than 110,000 immigrants that year as "refugees." In 1994, 112,573 "refugees" were welcomed to the U.S., though just one-sixth of them were recognized by the international relief community as "special needs refugees" requiring resettlement in a third country. Roger Winter, a refugee rights advocate working for the U.S. Committee for Refugees, has estimated that the cost of settling a refugee in the U.S. would cover the expenses of helping 500 refugees abroad.

Immigration Policy Must Be Overhauled

Clearly, current U.S. immigration policy needs to be overhauled. It is fiscally irresponsible toward U.S. taxpayers and economically unfair to American workers. It also is a disincentive for developing nations to learn to provide for their own citizens.

A study conducted by the Harwood Group showed that voters heading into the 1996 presidential election were more angry than ever with politicians in Washington for not addressing their major concerns—education, jobs, crime, and health care. According to a Roper poll released in February 1996, 54% of Americans want annual immigration to be less than 100,000 a year. That poll also showed the majority of blacks and Hispanics favor drastic reductions in immigration. A *Wall Street Journal*/NBC News poll published in March 1996 revealed that 52% of Americans favor banning all legal and illegal immigration for five years.

If the nation's leaders want to show the world that the U.S. practices democracy and if they are sincere about addressing voters' concerns, they immediately should support a five-year moratorium on legal immigration with an all-inclusive ceiling of 100,000 a year. The tens of billions of dollars saved annually in servicing fewer legal immigrants can be used to help balance budgets, fund measures to stop illegal immigration, invest in Head Start and public schools, and finance crime prevention programs. Such a moratorium would allow time to develop a long-term immigration policy that reflects economic realities and resource availability.

"The evidence shows that the problems attributed to immigration are false or greatly exaggerated."

LEGAL IMMIGRATION IS NOT A SERIOUS PROBLEM

Linda Chavez and John J. Miller

Linda Chavez and John J. Miller contend in the following viewpoint that many of the problems attributed to mass immigration are myths and exaggerations. They argue that immigrants have a positive effect on the nation's economy and future. Restricting immigration would only harm the nation's economy, Chavez and Miller assert. Chavez is president and Miller is vice president of the Center for Equal Opportunity in Washington, D.C.

As you read, consider the following questions:

1. What would be the result if American companies could not hire foreign-born workers, according to Chavez and Miller?
2. In the authors' opinion, how does immigration affect an area's unemployment rate?
3. According to Chavez and Miller, who pushes for bilingual education for the children of immigrants?

Reprinted from "The Immigration Myth," by Linda Chavez and John J. Miller, *Reader's Digest*, May 1996, by permission of *Reader's Digest* and the authors.

Americans like immigrants as individuals—the decent, hardworking Korean grocer on the corner, the Russian computer programmer who lives down the street or the Filipino nurse who works at the local hospital. But as a nation we don't seem to think much of immigration in general.

In a 1994 *Newsweek* survey, for example, half the public agreed that "immigrants are a burden because they take our jobs, housing and health care." Passions run high. "We are flooding areas of the country with millions of uneducated immigrants," complained one *Wall Street Journal* reader. They "take over, impose their culture and don't even try to assimilate."

Everyone agrees that we must police our borders against illegal immigrants. But some, including Presidential candidate Pat Buchanan, want to declare a moratorium on *all* immigration. Sen. Alan Simpson (R., Wyo.) has sponsored a bill that would reduce the number of legally admitted nonrefugee immigrants from 675,000 annually to 540,000.

Yet in sharp contrast to the prevailing rhetoric that feeds on misinformation, the evidence shows that the problems attributed to immigration are false or greatly exaggerated. In reality, today's immigrants contribute positively, in much the same way our own ancestors did. We would only hurt ourselves by shutting the door in their faces. It's time to debunk the myths that are clouding our public debate and policy.

MYTH: TODAY'S IMMIGRANTS ARE LESS EDUCATED THAN IN THE PAST

In fact, the educational level of immigrants has been increasing, not decreasing. About one-third of all new immigrants in 1960 had less than eight years of schooling. In the past decade, that proportion has dropped to one-quarter.

The percentage of immigrants with a college education and with advanced degrees has been increasing too. In the 1980s, for example, there were about 11,000 foreign-born engineers and scientists here. By 1992 that number had doubled.

An astonishing 40 percent of engineering doctorates at American universities in 1993 went to foreign-born professionals, who have become a vital force in the high-technology sectors critical to our future—telecommunications, biotechnology, chemicals and computers.

"How important are immigrants to my company?" asks T.J. Rodgers, president and CEO of Cypress Semiconductor, a manufacturer of high-performance computer chips in San Jose, Calif. "We would be out of business without them." In the research and development offices of the firm, pins on a world map represent employees' places of birth. Almost half lie outside American borders. Home countries include China, Ghana, India, Panama, the Philippines, Russia, Taiwan and Zimbabwe.

This is true of countless firms in America's computer industry. At giant Intel, maker of the Pentium processor used in millions of home computers, many of the people working on the Santa Clara–based company's top projects are immigrants. Take Indian-born Ryan Manepally. He co-developed the concept for a computer-to-computer video-conferencing product that would allow, for instance, doctors in different states to discuss X rays simultaneously. Intel CEO Andy Grove is from Hungary, and at least six of the company's 29 corporate vice presidents are also immigrants.

"Without immigrants, we would have to send work overseas," notes Anant Agrawal, Indian-born vice president of engineering at Sun Microsystems, Inc., a leading designer and manufacturer of workstations used for commercial and technical computing. "That certainly would not help the American economy."

MYTH: IMMIGRANTS STEAL JOBS FROM AMERICANS

Behind this myth, notes economist Julian Simon, is a basic fallacy: that the number of jobs is finite, and the more that immigrants occupy the fewer there are for others. Numerous studies dispute this myth. For instance, the Alexis de Tocqueville Institution in Arlington, Va., found that between 1960 and 1991, the ten states with the highest immigrant presence had a lower unemployment rate than the ten states with the lowest immigrant presence. Blacks—often portrayed as economic victims of immigration—were found to earn more when they live in cities with large immigrant populations than they do in cities with small ones.

Immigrants, notes Simon in a recent Cato Institute report on immigration, "make new jobs by spending their earnings on the output of other workers." What's more, less skilled immigrants take work Americans shun. IBP, Inc., near Garden City, Kan., operates the world's largest meatpacking plant. Workers at IBP are reasonably well paid—$7 to $10.35 per hour. Yet most of the workers on the "kill floor" there and at a nearby competitor, Monfort, are from Mexico or Southeast Asia. Meatpacking is the most hazardous job in the United States. Workers make several cuts on a carcass every few seconds for eight hours a day, six days a week. The kill floors can get wet with water and blood, and even the most experienced worker can fall or get cut. "There are jobs that native-born Americans simply won't do," says Steve Orozco, a program specialist at Job Service Center, a state agency in Garden City. "Meatpacking is one of them."

The 40 workers at the Dalma Dress Manufacturing Company in New York City are all foreign-born. "Hardly any Americans apply for a job here," says Tonia Sylla from Liberia, an 11-year veteran. "Even when they do, they don't last long." Says Dalma's owner, Armand DiPalma, "Immigrants are the only labor pool we have."

Half of the 800,000 garment workers in the United States are immigrants, part of a $120-billion industry. If they were not doing the work, the jobs would probably move overseas.

"Every time you see a 'Made in the USA' label on a piece of clothing," says Bruce Herman of the Garment Industry Development Corporation, "chances are you can thank an immigrant."

MYTH: IMMIGRANTS ARE WELFARE MOOCHERS

Because immigrants admitted as refugees are guaranteed cash and medical assistance by federal law, the proportion of foreign-born on welfare is 6.6 percent, versus 4.9 percent of native-born. However, only 5.1 percent of nonrefugee working-age immigrants—the vast majority of legally admitted foreign-born—receive welfare benefits, compared with 5.3 percent of working-age native-born.

In reality, the work ethic of today's immigrants is just as strong as that of the Irish, Italians and Poles of yesteryear. According to the 1990 census, foreign-born males have a 77 percent labor-force participation rate, compared with 74 percent for native-born Americans. Hispanics have the highest rate of any group, 83 percent.

No doubt, too, many immigrants receive government benefits. However, the problem is not the immigrants but our overgenerous welfare state. California, for example, burdened as it is by federally mandated programs, is also laden with state-sponsored aid programs. The strain on the state's taxpayers boiled over in 1994 when Proposition 187, a ballot measure that denies benefits to illegal immigrants, passed by a huge margin.

Texas, on the other hand, spends less on welfare. It has taken in millions of immigrants in recent years without the public backlash. Gov. George W. Bush opposes laws modeled on Proposition 187, which have gone nowhere in the Texas legislature.

"Immigrants have the determination to succeed," declares Patricia Charlton, who arrived penniless from Jamaica in 1981 and started work at a McDonald's in Manhattan. She worked her way up, eventually being named a regional Manager of the Year. She's married, owns a house and has a child in private school.

Like Charlton, immigrants often start on the lowest rungs of the economic ladder and move up. Typically, their household incomes reach parity with the native-born after about ten years, according to census figures.

IMMIGRANTS ARE PRODUCTIVE

Numerous studies have found that immigrants actually *create* more jobs than they fill. The jobs immigrants take are of course easier to see, but immigrants are often highly productive, run their own businesses and employ both immigrants and citizens. One study found that Mexican immigration to Los Angeles County between 1970 and 1980 was responsible for 78,000 new jobs. Governor Mario Cuomo reports that immigrants own more than 40,000 companies in New York, which provide thousands of jobs and $3.5 billion to the state's economy every year.

David Cole, *Nation*, October 17, 1994.

"Often immigrant-owned businesses invest in inner cities where rents are cheap, becoming a revitalizing force there," says Stephen N. Solarsh, a New York City business and real-estate adviser to many immigrant-owned businesses. Korean immigrant Kim Suk Su, for example, currently owns property in some of the worst areas in Brooklyn, N.Y. Each was vacant when he bought it, but today most are back on the tax rolls.

Koreans Choi Duckchun and his wife, Hae Su, work seven days a week at their New York City delicatessen, paying a $15,800 monthly rent and a $10,000 monthly payroll, while trying to save enough to eventually send their three young children to college. It's a struggle, and crime is a problem. Nevertheless, their hard work pays off. "In Korea, money and politics determine everything," Choi says. "Here it's the land of opportunity."

There is one final irony in the charge that immigrants are welfare moochers. Most immigrants arrive in their prime working years, their late 20s. "The payroll taxes of these young immigrants," notes economist Simon, "help underwrite the Social Security checks of America's senior citizens."

MYTH: IMMIGRANTS DON'T WANT TO ASSIMILATE

Language is the key issue for assimilation, and self-interest impels most foreign-born to learn ours quickly—unless government gets in the way.

"I didn't speak any English when I came here in 1984," says

Miguel Angel Rivera, who lives in Baltimore. "I didn't need to because I was washing dishes and busing tables."

Then the Salvadoran decided to become a waiter. "I started working the floor and picked up English from the customers," he says.

Today Rivera is fluent. He also owns and operates Baltimore's Restaurante San Luis, which specializes in Chinese and Salvadoran cuisine. "I have no problem communicating with any of my customers," he says.

Although many immigrants don't speak a word of English when they arrive here, most recognize that learning it is the key to their economic success. A study of Southeast Asian refugees in Houston found that fluent English speakers earned almost three times as much money as those who only spoke a few words.

Progress might even be faster among the young were it not for bilingual education, which can reinforce the native tongue and delay the learning of English for years. Failed policies such as bilingual education and multicultural curricula are not being demanded by Mexican laborers or Chinese waiters. Instead they are being rammed down immigrants' throats by federal, state and local governments, at the behest of native-born political activists and bureaucrats.

Culturally, immigrants believe in the melting pot and want to join the mainstream. Ninety percent of Hispanics are "proud" or "very proud" of the United States, according to a recent Latino National Political Survey.

Greg Gourley teaches citizenship classes at several Seattle-area community colleges. To become citizens, immigrants must speak, read and write in English, and pass an exam about U.S. history and government. The test is not easy. "If they didn't want to be Americans, they wouldn't be here," Gourley says. "We've got a waiting list a mile long."

Not every politician has jumped on the anti-immigration bandwagon. Many, including House Majority Leader Dick Armey (R., Texas), Sen. Joe Lieberman (D., Conn.) and Gov. George Pataki (R., N.Y.), see through the myths, and understand that the United States gains when legal immigrants arrive. As Sen. Spencer Abraham (R., Mich.) says, "We should not shut the door to people yearning to be free and to build a better life for themselves and their families."

that growing numbers of nonwhites threaten our [?] [P]atrick Buchanan) or our gene pool (Charles Mur-[?] [m]ore, the obsession with illegal immigration on the [?] [polit]icians like Pete Wilson evades the main issue. Each [?] [300,00]0 to 400,000 illegal immigrants arrive in the U.S. [?] [a fract]ion of the roughly 1 million legal immigrants who [?] [perm]anent residence each year. We can and should crack [?] [on ill]egal immigration—with a stronger border patrol, [?] [a] computerized national employment verification [?] [but] legal immigration represents the greater threat to [?] [wa]ges and unions.

[?] legal immigration is a perfectly legitimate liberal [?] "[l]iberal" means protecting the interests of ordinary [?] [worki]ng Americans. Unfortunately, for thirty years the [?] [cratic] Party has not acted like a liberal or social-democratic [?] [It] acted as a coalition of ethnic patronage machines [?] [seekin]g to enlarge the numbers of its group eligible for af-[?] [tive a]ction) and affluent white social liberals (whose [?] [in] many cases depend on a supporting cast of low-[?] [paid] American maids and nannies). Unlike free-market [?] [tiv]es, who can at least invoke a principled libertarian [?] [id]eal, pro-immigration liberals have no theory, merely the [?] ["p]oetry" of which Strout wrote—and the N-word (na-[?] [tivism]). now that majorities of black Americans and even a [?] [majo]rity of Hispanics, according to a Roper poll commis-[?] [sioned by] Negative Population Growth Institute, support reduc-[?] [immi]gration to less than 300,000 a year, it will no longer [?] [accu]se all supporters of immigration reform of racism and [?] [xenophob]ia.

[FA]CTS

[?] concluded in a critique of immigration policy back in [?] [pe]ople must face facts, whether they like them or not." A [?] [ma]jority of liberal Democrats, including Wisconsin Con-[?] [gressman] David Obey, have done so, signing on as cosponsors of [?] [immi]gration reform bills introduced by Alan Simpson in the [?] [Senate an]d Lamar Smith in the House. Though the bills wisely [?] [focus] on extended-family reunification—a Ponzi scheme that [?] [has resul]ted in escalating immigrant numbers—they would re-[?] [duce lega]l immigration by only a third, to about 700,000 a year. [?] [That's] still much too high. The numerical cap envisioned by [?] [the orig]inal Kennedy-Johnson reform in 1965—290,000 a [?] [year—w]ould do more to bring U.S. population growth in line [?] [with oth]er developed countries and to raise U.S. wages, particu-

> *"We can and should crack down on illegal immigration . . . but legal immigration represents the greater threat to American wages and unions."*

LEGAL IMMIGRATION HARMS AMERICAN WORKERS

Michael Lind

Mass immigration reduces wages among unskilled workers and drives low-income workers from high-immigration areas, argues Michael Lind in the following viewpoint. He maintains that middle- and working-class Americans made their greatest economic gains during eras of restricted immigration. Reducing the number of legal immigrants would protect the interests of American wage-earners, Lind concludes. Lind is a senior editor for the *New Republic*, a liberal weekly political magazine.

As you read, consider the following questions:

1. What is the Census Bureau's new estimate of the U.S. population in 2080, as cited by Lind?
2. What is the constitutional amendment proposed by the *Wall Street Journal*, according to Lind?
3. In the author's opinion, how many immigrants should be permitted in the United States each year?

Reprinted from "Huddled Excesses," by Michael Lind, *New Republic*, April 1, 1996, by permission of the *New Republic*; ©1996, The New Republic, Inc.

Sooner or later America must face reality. It is going to be painful. . . . [W]hat America is fighting is a piece of poetry. . . . The poetry is thrilling. It is on the Statue of Liberty: "Give me your tired, your poor, your huddled masses yearning to breathe free. . . ." The trouble is that huddled masses need jobs.

Patrick Buchanan? No, Richard Strout, the eminent liberal journalist who wrote this column for several decades. Since Strout wrote those words in 1980, more than 10 million people have immigrated to the United States legally. The number of new immigrants, and their higher-than-average birthrate, forced the Census Bureau to revise its 1989 estimate of U.S. population in 2080 upward, by an additional 100 *million*—to 400 million.

DECLINING WAGES

But it is not numbers alone that should convert liberal immigration defenders. As Strout observed, the "huddled masses need jobs." According to a 1995 Bureau of Labor Statistics study, competition with immigrants has accounted for roughly half the recent decline in wages among unskilled American workers. According to University of Michigan demographer William Frey, competition for jobs with poorly paid Latin American and Asian immigrants is driving low-income whites and blacks out of high-immigration states like California and high-immigration cities like New York. No wonder Steve Forbes and Dick Armey favor high levels of immigration, and *The Wall Street Journal* has proposed a five-word amendment to the U.S. Constitution—"There shall be open borders." It's great for business.

But not so great for poor Americans. And they're not the only ones under threat. U.S. companies can legally hire 140,000 *skilled* foreign workers each year. Business lobbyists have claimed that the U.S. computer industry needs a neverending supply of East Asian and Indian scientists because there are not enough Americans able to do the work. Really? Why can't American industry train native and naturalized citizens for high-tech jobs? Some companies do the reverse. In 1994, the American International Group Insurance Company fired more than 250 American computer programmers and replaced them with Indian workers brought in under the H-1B visa program (which allows firms to pay only the foreign prevailing wage plus a living allowance). To add insult to injury, the laid-off workers, on pain of losing their severance pay, were forced to train their foreign replacements for sixty days.

The greatest gains in income by the American middle and working classes, both white and black, took place during the era

of immigration restrictio
coincidentally, this was al
which is inevitably hampe
a workforce divided by e
golden age of public sup
anti-poverty efforts. Coinci
and egalitarian countries in
homogeneous nation-state
grants, like those of norther
rate paternalism substitutes
of social justice and nationa
pelling in the modern U.S., v
more likely than native-born
fits. (In Chinese-speaking Asia
potential immigrants how to
Income] and other benefits of

NO ECONOMIC RATIONALE

Economists have usually focuse
gration—that is, are immigrant
they contribute? It's been a fierc
clear that the pessimists have w
deed a net fiscal burden. . . .

The United States has had mas
great wave was at the beginning
had the welfare state, from the 1
immigration and the welfare st
combination can work.

For example, up to 40 percent of
Ellis Island at the turn of the centu
had to. If they failed in the workfo
assistance. But now, if immigrants
welfare. So they have been stayin
home. The dynamic has fundamenta

This problem has been made worse
the 1965 Immigration Act. The act u
from the needs of the American eco
called "family reunification" over i
employers wanted. In 1992, only 13
gal admissions were "employment-ba

Peter Brimelowe, *American Legion,* July 1997.

There is, then, a liberal case for in
has nothing to do with the absurd an

conservatives
civilization (
ray). What's
part of politi
year, 300,00
to stay, a frac
take up pern
down on ill
fences and
system—bu
American w
Reducing
cause—if "
wage-earni
Democratic
party. It ha
(each seeki
firmative
lifestyles i
wage Latin
conservati
viewpoint
"piece of
tivist). Bu
slight maj
sioned by
ing immi
do to accu
xenophob

FACING F

As Strout
1981, "P
brave mi
gressmar
the imm
Senate a
cut back
has resu
duce leg
That'
the ori
year—
with ot

larly at the bottom of the income scale. Yet there would still be room for plenty of humanitarian refugees, spouses and children of Mexican-American citizens, Taiwanese grad students and English journalists. Though the U.S. would no longer take half the world's legal immigrants, we would still have the world's most generous immigration policy. . . .

Genuine liberals should unite with populist conservatives to reform an immigration policy that benefits few Americans other than exploitative employers. It is easy to talk in poetry. But it is necessary to govern in prose.

"It is absurd to suggest that immigration is the source of ethnic tension in the American work force."

LEGAL IMMIGRATION DOES NOT HARM AMERICAN WORKERS

Charles Lane

In a rebuttal to *New Republic* senior editor Michael Lind, Charles Lane, also a *New Republic* senior editor, contends that the number of immigrants is much smaller now than it was when U.S. immigration peaked in the early twentieth century. Moreover, Lane argues, it is absurd to believe that immigration is responsible for racial tensions in the workforce or for the rise and fall of labor unions. Blaming America's problems on immigrants is xenophobic, Lane asserts.

As you read, consider the following questions:

1. What was the immigration rate per thousand inhabitants between 1970 and 1990, according to Lind, as cited by Lane?
2. In the author's opinion, why is it absurd to blame racial tensions in the workforce on immigration?
3. Why is Lind's theory that the most homogenous countries are the most egalitarian mistaken, according to Lane?

Reprinted from "Grandfathered In," by Charles Lane, *New Republic*, April 8, 1996, by permission of the *New Republic*; ©1996, The New Republic, Inc.

Recently my 94-year-old grandfather showed me the Sabbath candlesticks his mother brought over on the boat from Poland eight-and-a-half decades ago. Those treasured items, wrapped in a bundle of sheets, were the Lanes' only possessions when—still named Levine—they first set foot on these shores. Intent on being a "real" American, my grandfather enlisted in World War I and spent the next forty years in the Army. As a military retiree since 1955, his pension receipts have defied actuarial gravity. Has America gotten more out of my grandfather than it paid in? I like to think so, especially since I'd never have been born if he hadn't come. At the very least, his story, and millions like it, should give some pause to immigration restrictionists.

An Unpersuasive Argument

My colleague Michael Lind knows exactly how many immigrants America needs: 700,000 entrants a year would be "much too high," he opined in the April 1, 1996, *New Republic*, whereas 290,000 would help to "bring U.S. population growth in line with other developed countries and to raise U.S. wages. . . ." As a restrictionist brief, Lind's bolster-the-little-guy argument is superficially more palatable than [conservative presidential candidate] Pat Buchanan's raw Eurocentrism. Ultimately, however, it is no more persuasive. For starters, Lind should calm down about the magnitude of what he twice refers to as the "threat" of immigration. The influx of immigrants per thousand U.S. inhabitants lags far behind the pace set in the nineteenth century by the Irish, Germans and Chinese who built much of this country. Between 1901 and 1910, the rate peaked at 10.4 immigrants per 1,000 inhabitants. Between 1970 and 1990, the inflow averaged about a fourth of that. According to Lind, the latest Bureau of Labor Statistics research proves that half of a "recent" (unspecified) decrease in unskilled workers' wages is due to immigration. I've seen other studies that "prove" immigrants' spending and investment creates new jobs or that their tax payments outweigh their welfare take. The question of whether immigration is good or bad for the American economy is like the question of whether the federal budget deficit is good or bad for the American economy: it all depends on your frame of reference. Do the benefits to today's generations from deficit spending outweigh the probably large but unknown costs to tomorrow's generations? If you're collecting Social Security today, you're more likely to say yes; if you're hoping to collect it forty years from now, you might say no. The purported harm to American wages from immigration—an argument restrictionists have been making since the 1850s—doesn't settle the more fateful question of whether the country generally will be better off a generation hence. Surely Lind doesn't mean to suggest that it was a mistake to admit all those scruffy Europeans a century ago.

WITH IMMIGRANT WORKERS

WITHOUT IMMIGRANT WORKERS

Paul Conrad. Copyright ©1994 Los Angeles Times Syndicate. Reprinted with permission.

He does claim that the period between the 1920s and the 1960s was a golden immigration-free age during which "[t]he greatest gains in income by the American middle and working classes, both white and black, took place. . . ." (I'm not so sure that any "working-class" windfall would justify the injury done to American democracy by the explicitly racist Immigration Act of 1924, which ushered in this golden era.) Lind's sweeping causal insinuation simply ignores such intervening economic watersheds as the mechanization of Southern agriculture and the northward migration of blacks or the erection of a vast peacetime military establishment. Besides, his reading of the data is debatable. The 1930s were marked by the slowest immigration and the deepest mass poverty in American history. The economic expansion of the 1940s and 1950s actually coincided with a steady *increase* in the rate of immigration.

IMMIGRATION AND UNIONS

At times, Lind veers dangerously close to the very Buchananism he elsewhere attacks. "[M]ass immigration produces a work force [which is] divided by ethnicity" and hence more difficult to unionize, he argues. It is absurd to suggest that immigration is the source of ethnic tension in the American work force, and that, without it, workers might link arms at last. The American labor force has been ethnically divided since the day Africans were first brought here as slaves; black-white conflict alone would continue to undermine working-class solidarity even if we never admitted another immigrant. Of course, in America, modern trade unionism is itself largely a European import. That said, the ebb and flow of unionism has depended more on technology, trade and government labor policies than on trends in immigration. In the period Lind is talking about, the mandatory union dues checkoff, imposed by FDR [Franklin D. Roosevelt] as a political reward to the CIO [Congress of Industrial Organizations]during World War II, was by far the biggest spur to unionization.

Lind gives the game away when he says that "[t]he most generous and egalitarian countries in modern times have been culturally homogeneous nation-states admitting few or no poor immigrants, like those of northern Europe and Japan." Why is Japan, with its rigid social hierarchy and subordinated women, more "egalitarian" than the U.S.? Actually, Germany (millions of Turkish *Gastarbeiter*) and Japan (large unacknowledged populations of Korean-origin non-citizens and Filipina bar girls) are societies that have hypocritically pretended not to need or allow immigration, while importing disenfranchised foreigners to do their dirty work. America, like the rest of the developed world, does face a genuine dilemma: the population of poorer countries is growing far faster than ours is, and thus a vast pool of labor is arising to compete with Americans either as immigrants here or workers at home, whether we like it or not. But let Japan and Europe try to stick their fingers in the dike. The flexibility and adaptability of American capitalism mean (a) that we can find arrangements of comparative advantage with developing countries whereby they do the tasks America outgrows and (b) that we can continue to profit from absorbing a reasonably large share of the brightest and most adventuresome of their excess population.

XENOPHOBIA

Lind calls David Obey and other liberals who have joined the congressional move for lower ceilings on legal immigration "a brave minority," standing up to an elite that rationalizes its addiction to cheap Guatemalan help with sentimental "poetry" about the Statue of Liberty. As if it's ever taken much bravery to blame this country's ills on outsiders! In a nation where practically everyone is descended from an immigrant, a tolerant attitude toward immigration is merely an appropriate expression of civic humility. I once made this argument to my grandfather, of all people, as we were driving through one of Washington's more ethnically diverse areas. He was muttering about the odd-looking Ethiopians and Salvadorans he saw through the window. "People used to say the same thing when they saw you in New York seventy years ago," I countered. "That was different," he huffed. "We wanted to assimilate." Whereupon I dropped the subject. But I do recall thinking that one of those Salvadorans will probably have the same absurd dialogue with his grandson sixty years from now.

"These hundreds of thousands of
illegal aliens pose a severe strain on
the U.S. welfare and health care
facilities."

ILLEGAL IMMIGRATION HARMS THE UNITED STATES

G. Russell Evans

In the following viewpoint, G. Russell Evans argues that illegal immigration places a severe strain on the U.S. economy and on the health care and welfare systems. He contends that illegal immigrants compete with American workers for jobs and wages. In addition, giving illegal aliens the right to vote, as is done in some jurisdictions, is contrary to the rights and privileges of citizenship, Evans maintains, and will lead to contentious ethnic conflict. Evans is a retired captain in the U.S. Coast Guard.

As you read, consider the following questions:

1. Reports that allege there is no competition between illegal immigrants and American workers for jobs omit what fact, according to Evans?
2. On what basis do immigration supporters defend an illegal alien's right to vote, as cited by Evans?
3. In the author's opinion, what is happening to American lands in the Southwest?

Reprinted from "The Crisis of Illegal Immigration," by G. Russell Evans, *Conservative Review*, March/April 1994, by permission of the *Conservative Review*.

The ever-worsening crisis of illegal immigration is brushed aside by some as inconsequential. One says, "The illegals are just taking jobs that Americans don't want; and, besides, aren't we the world's melting pot?"

Not quite. The arguments that illegal immigrants take low-paying labor and service jobs that Americans are unwilling to accept and that illegal aliens do not increase unemployment is countered by several facts:

(1) The abundance of illegal workers simply gives employers the opportunity to reduce wages and downgrade working conditions. Therefore, these low-paying jobs are the consequence of illegal immigrants, not the cause, and the result is to depress wages. This situation discourages the creation of better-paying jobs and automation in America.

(2) Reports that allege there is no job competition between illegal workers and Americans omit the fact that American workers, as a general rule, move out of areas where the illegals settle. According to Cornell University labor specialist Vernon Briggs, an example is Los Angeles, where, 20 years ago, many black Americans were employed in building maintenance jobs. Then the illegals moved in, many blacks moved out, and wages dropped 40 percent.

(3) Another example shows direct competition between illegal aliens and American workers. Rice University analyst Donald Huddle found that one-third of construction workers in Houston were illegals holding down good-paying jobs that otherwise would have gone to American workers. Dr. Huddle noted that the salaries of these illegals "debunk the notion that illegal aliens are taking only those jobs that Americans don't want because they are so low paid."

THOUSANDS OF ILLEGAL ALIENS DAILY

On a TV newscast, an Immigration and Naturalization Service (INS) spokesman stated that between two and three thousand illegal aliens daily cross the border in San Diego County, California. Some are captured and set free on their promise to return for a deportation hearing. Many escape. If an alien fails to appear at a deportation hearing, he or she can be deported in *absentia* and disqualified from gaining re-entry for five years. The INS, however, in implementing this law, has difficulty in keeping tabs on those released and in determining who is a flight risk and who may be a threat to society.

Needless to say, these hundreds of thousands of illegal aliens pose a severe strain on the U.S. welfare and health care facilities.

Already, the United States has the most liberal *legal* immigration policy in the world, and with illegals added, the stress on the national budget is terrific.

Congressional laws make these illegals eligible for several kinds of welfare, as well as for educational and health care programs. Opposition to the illegal immigrants cannot be dismissed with charges of racism and other buzz words to scare off debate. The illegals are here, still coming, and our politicians seem in some cases to relish the thought.

AN ABSURDLY LOW ESTIMATE

Border patrol field agents calculate that three aliens escape apprehension for every one caught. This is a conservative estimate, as most agents say the rate is more likely five to one. Yet the INS estimate of illegal border crossers comes out to only 69 illegal aliens each day. Why would the United States be putting 4,000 Border Patrol agents on the southern land border in 1995, an increase of 1,000 agents over 1994, if the number of border crossers were so small? The figure, which reflects the absurdity of the INS estimate, does not include illegal aliens crossing the Canadian land border or arriving at airports, seaports, or other coastal landings. The only logical conclusion is that *more* than 300,000 illegal aliens are permanently entering the U.S. each year—*many more*.

James H. Walsh, *Social Contract*, Winter 1995–1996.

Congress has not provided the wherewithal to the Border Patrol to enforce the immigration laws. Instead, in 1986, Congress provided amnesty to over three million illegal aliens already here, thereby making it *legal* for these three million to bring in children and parents, for a grand total of perhaps nine million more immigrants, placing further stress on the national budget and job market.

Cheap labor is one of the obvious uses of illegal aliens. Employers are required to check the documentation of workers to prove the legal right to jobs, but counterfeit documentation has largely thwarted this program. The INS does not have the facilities to enforce this law, and some say, "Lawmakers don't really want them enforced" (*Border Watch*, June 1992, newsletter of the American Immigration Control Foundation).

ILLEGALS AND THE RIGHT TO VOTE

Perhaps our Congress wants the votes of the illegal immigrants. Yes, in Takoma Park, Maryland, the illegals can vote. . . . Supporters of voting rights for illegals claim that non-citizens should be allowed to vote because they pay taxes. Professor Jamin B. Raskin of American University believes that alien voting should be picked up by large cities "like Los Angeles, Houston, Washington and New York . . . to strengthen American democracy by including in the crucial processes of local government many hundreds of thousands of people born elsewhere." What kind of logic is this?

This radical idea of Jamin Raskin is contrary to the concept of American citizenship, one of the most precious privileges of which is the right to vote.

Observers abroad are quite critical of our immigration policies, and one from Honduras wrote, "The United States is doomed." Do we need advice from the Japanese? Yuji Aida of the University of Kyoto warns that soon the U.S. will have to deal with "contentious ethnic groups demanding autonomy and political independence." He adds, "[I]t is only a matter of time before U.S. minority groups espouse self-determination. When that happens, the country may become ungovernable." As an analogy, he suggests the former Soviet Union, now disintegrated into ethnic states.

The Hispanization of America

The Mexican view on the "Hispanization of America" is given by Raymundo Riva Palacio, correspondent for the Mexico City *Excelsior*. He reports that counties in Arizona, New Mexico, Texas and California are returning to what they were before: *Mexican lands*. He added: No U.S. immigration laws, as presently conceived, will change the Hispanization of the American Southwest.

Are we to permit our Congress to allow this surrender of the right to vote to illegal aliens? If patriotism is indeed the last refuge of a scoundrel, the laxity in controlling illegal aliens must be the first refuge for unscrupulous politicians anxious for more votes.

> "The number of Mexicans living
> illegally in this country is smaller
> than has been widely assumed."

THE EXTENT OF ILLEGAL IMMIGRATION IS EXAGGERATED

Frank del Olmo

In the following viewpoint, Frank del Olmo reports on a U.S.-Mexican study that found that the number of illegal Mexican immigrants in the United States is much lower than previously was believed. In addition, the study concludes that as the Mexican economy improves, the number of future illegal immigrants will continue to fall. Del Olmo contends that the easing of the illegal immigration crisis from Mexico is a natural result of letting the free market operate without human controls; imposing government solutions to prevent short-term illegal immigration will only have a deleterious effect on long-term immigration policy. Del Olmo is a columnist and assistant to the editor at the *Los Angeles Times*.

As you read, consider the following questions:

1. According to the binational study cited by del Olmo, how many illegal Mexican immigrants enter the United States each year?
2. What three "push" factors are expected to change in the future, according to the study cited by the author?
3. In del Olmo's opinion, who should be allowed to immigrate easily to the United States?

When it comes to the carefully measured use of language, academic researchers are outdone only by diplomats. So you can just imagine the cautious language of a document written by both.

The "Binational Study of Migration Between Mexico and the United States" is just such a report, right down to its aptly bureaucratic title. Yet it comes to conclusions that are sure to be controversial. Still, any controversy that this calm, deliberately written study stirs up will be less a reflection of the research itself than of how immigration has been turned into a "hot button" issue by political demagogues.

In California and the rest of the Southwest, the focus of anti-immigrant rhetoric is the generations-old migration of Mexican workers into this country. Three years ago, to help calm an increasingly hysterical debate, the U.S. and Mexican governments commissioned 20 migration experts (10 from each country) to conduct an independent, collaborative survey of the current state of that historic flow.

The Mexican side of the survey was overseen by that country's foreign ministry. The U.S. research was authorized by the Commission on Immigration Reform, a nine-member body that advises Congress on immigration issues. Formerly headed by Barbara Jordan, the late congresswoman from Texas, the commission is now headed by former Education Secretary Shirley Hufstedler, a prominent Los Angeles attorney. The binational study is only the latest admirable effort by the Jordan/Hufstedler commission to bring reasoned discourse to an emotionally charged issue.

The study's results were made public in September 1997 and most news reports focused on a finding that the number of Mexicans living illegally in this country is smaller than has been widely assumed. Using U.S. and Mexican census data and related statistics, researchers estimate that roughly 105,000 Mexicans have settled illegally in this country each year since 1990, far fewer than the millions claimed by anti-immigrant politicians like Pat Buchanan.

A SHARP DROP IN IMMIGRATION NUMBERS

But to my way of thinking, the binational study's most important conclusion focuses on the future flow of migrants from Mexico *al norte*. It points to a far more optimistic scenario than most Americans might expect.

"There is reason to believe," the report states, "that the currently high levels of migration may represent a 'hump' or peak. . . .

Within the next decade, changes in Mexican demographics and other structural changes should begin to reduce emigration pressures."

First, the researchers conclude that the "push factors" that send Mexicans abroad looking for work are weakening. The cohort in the Mexican population most likely to migrate, workers between 15 and 44 years old, will decline from 1.05 million in 1996 to 430,000 by 2010. The ambitious economic liberalization Mexico began in 1990 will produce the jobs to keep those workers at home, if the nation achieves its economic goal of a 5% annual growth rate. Even with a growth rate of 3% (the figure the study used) almost 800,000 new jobs will be generated by 2005.

Stop Scapegoating Illegal Immigrants

Arguing that illegal immigrants are the source of unemployment, higher taxes, and spiraling healthcare and social service costs . . . flies in the face of well-documented studies. For example, a 1992 U.S. Department of Justice study found that less than 1% of immigrants legalized under the 1986 amnesty had received general assistance, Social Security, SSI, worker's compensation or unemployment insurance. Less than one-half of 1% received food stamps or AFDC. As for jobs, it is well known that California's agriculture industry is dependent on immigrants, who overwhelmingly work at jobs that most U.S. citizens will not take because of the low pay, lack of benefits, and horrendous working conditions.

Rethinking Schools, Autumn 1994.

The researchers also assume the "pull factors" in the U.S. economy that lure foreign workers here will weaken due to a recent increase in minimum wages that should make some menial jobs more attractive to U.S. citizens and an "increased supply of low-skilled U.S. residents shifted out of welfare programs."

The study's authors are exceedingly cautious in suggesting future policies. They suggest that "the study findings argue for increased dialogue and forward-looking consultative mechanisms to facilitate bilateral cooperation in finding mutually beneficial solutions to unauthorized migration."

Fine. But let me put in my own, admittedly undiplomatic words what we should get out of this fine study:

We got ourselves all worked up over a problem that pretty much is solving itself, which is what usually happens when human nature and the free market are allowed to operate unfettered by government-imposed controls. We may not be over the demographic hump yet, but we can see light at the end of the tunnel.

Since our most notorious immigration challenge soon will be eased, Congress must not overreact to short-term border problems by taking the harsh steps put forward as "solutions" by political charlatans like Buchanan. That would include further militarizing our borders and barring the children of illegal immigrants from becoming U.S. citizens.

Once Congress looks beyond the Mexican border, it can focus on long-term immigration challenges. The Jordan/Hufstedler commission has already pointed to some, such as ensuring that the foreigners we will want and need—investors, inventors, artists and the like—can immigrate with a minimum of hassle. For if the binational study and the other thoughtful research the commission has overseen are a guide, we can count on remaining a "nation of immigrants" well into the next century.

| "Immigrant participation in welfare programs is on the rise."

IMMIGRANTS ABUSE THE WELFARE SYSTEM

George Borjas

George Borjas is a professor of public policy at the John F. Kennedy School of Government, Harvard University, and the author of numerous articles on immigration. In the following viewpoint, Borjas argues that more and more immigrants to the United States are participating in welfare programs for longer periods of time, and are receiving benefits disproportionate to their numbers. Welfare payments add to the costs and economic burdens of immigration, Borjas contends, and could influence immigrants' decisions concerning work and immigration.

As you read, consider the following questions:

1. According to Borjas, how many immigrant households received cash benefits from welfare programs in 1990?
2. Counting all types of welfare payments, what percentage of immigrant households participated in means-tested programs, according to the author?
3. Why is the argument that the welfare problem is caused by refugee/elderly immigrants factually incorrect, in Borjas's opinion?

Reprinted from "The Welfare Magnet," by George Borjas, *National Review*, March 11, 1996, by permission of the author.

The evidence has become overwhelming: immigrant participation in welfare programs is on the rise. In 1970, immigrant households were slightly less likely than native households to receive cash benefits like AFDC (Aid to Families with Dependent Children) or SSI (Supplementary Security Income). By 1990, immigrant households were more likely to receive such cash benefits (9.1 per cent v. 7.4 per cent). Pro-immigration lobbyists are increasingly falling back on the excuse that this immigrant-native "welfare gap" is attributable solely to refugees and/or elderly immigrants; or that the gap is not numerically large. (Proportionately, it's "only" 23 per cent.)

But the Census does not provide any information about the use of noncash transfers. These are programs like Food Stamps, Medicaid, housing subsidies, and the myriad of other subsidies that make up the modern welfare state. And noncash transfers comprise over three quarters of the cost of all means-tested entitlement programs. In 1991, the value of these noncash transfers totaled about $140 billion.

THE SIPP DATA

Recently available data help provide a more complete picture. The Survey of Income and Program Participation (SIPP) samples randomly selected households about their involvement in virtually all means-tested programs. From this, the proportion of immigrant households that receive benefits from any particular program can be calculated.

The results are striking. The "welfare gap" between immigrants and natives is much larger when noncash transfers are included [see table]. Taking all types of welfare together, immigrant participation is 20.7 per cent. For native-born households, it's only 14.1 per cent—a gap of 6.6 percentage points (proportionately, 47 per cent).

And the SIPP data also indicate that immigrants spend a relatively large fraction of their time participating in some means-tested program. In other words, the "welfare gap" does not occur because many immigrant households receive assistance for a short time, but because a significant proportion—more than the native-born—receive assistance for the long haul.

ETHNIC NETWORKS

Finally, the SIPP data show that the types of welfare benefits received by particular immigrant groups influence the type of welfare benefits received by later immigrants from the same group. Implication: there appear to be networks operating within ethnic communities which transmit information about the availability of particular types of welfare to new arrivals.

The results are even more striking in detail. Immigrants are more likely to participate in practically every one of the major means-tested programs. In the early 1990s, the typical immigrant family household had a 4.4 per cent probability of receiving AFDC, v. 2.9 per cent of native-born families. [Further details in the table.]

And that overall "welfare gap" becomes even wider if immigrant families are compared to non-Hispanic white native-born households. Immigrants are almost twice as likely to receive some type of assistance—20.7 per cent v. 10.5 per cent.

AVERAGE MONTHLY PROBABILITY OF RECEIVING BENEFITS IN EARLY 1990s

Type of Benefit	Immigrant Households	Native Households
Cash Programs:		
Aid to Families with Dependent Children (AFDC)	4.4	2.9
Supplemental Security Income (SSI)	6.5	3.7
General Assistance	0.8	0.6
Noncash Programs:		
Medicaid	15.4	9.4
Food Stamps	9.2	6.5
Supplemental Food Program for Women, Infants, and Children (WIC)	3.0	2.0
Energy Assistance	2.1	2.3
Housing Assistance (public housing or low-rent subsidies)	5.6	4.4
School Breakfasts and Lunches (free or reduced price)	12.5	6.2
Summary:		
Receive Cash Benefits, Medicaid, Food Stamps, WIC, Energy Assistance, or Housing Assistance	20.7	14.1

George J. Borjas and Lynette Hilton, *Quarterly Journal of Economics*, May 1996.

The SIPP data also allow us to calculate the dollar value of the benefits disbursed to immigrant households, as compared to the native-born. In the early 1990s, 8 per cent of households were foreign-born. These immigrant households accounted for 13.8 per cent of the cost of the programs. They cost almost 75 per cent more than their representation in the population.

The disproportionate disbursement of benefits to immigrant households is particularly acute in California, a state which has both a lot of immigrants and very generous welfare programs. Immigrants make up only 21 per cent of the households in California. But these households consume 39.5 per cent of all the benefit dollars distributed in the state. It is not too much of an exaggeration to say that the welfare problem in California is on the verge of becoming an immigrant problem.

The pattern holds for other states. In Texas, where 8.9 per cent of households are immigrant but which has less generous welfare, immigrants receive 22 per cent of benefits distributed. In New York State, 16 per cent of the households are immigrant. They receive 22.2 per cent of benefits.

LONG-TERM TRACKING

The SIPP data track households over a 32-month period. This allows us to determine if immigrant welfare participation is temporary—perhaps the result of dislocation and adjustment—or long-term and possibly permanent.

The evidence is disturbing. During the early 1990s, nearly a third (31.3 per cent) of immigrant households participated in welfare programs at some point in the tracking period. Only just over a fifth (22.7 per cent) of native-born households did so. And 10.3 per cent of immigrant households received benefits through the *entire* period, v. 7.3 per cent of native-born households.

Because the Bureau of the Census began to collect the SIPP data in 1984, we can use it to assess if there have been any noticeable changes in immigrant welfare use. It turns out there has been a very rapid rise.

During the mid-1980s, the probability that an immigrant household received some type of assistance was 17.7 per cent v. 14.6 per cent for natives, a gap of 3.1 percentage points. By the early 1990s, recipient immigrant households had risen to 20.7 per cent, v. 14.1 per cent for natives. The immigrant-native "welfare gap," therefore, more than doubled in less than a decade.

Thus immigrants are not only more likely to have some exposure to the welfare system; they are also more likely to be "permanent" recipients. And the trend is getting worse. Unless eligibility requirements are made much more stringent, much of the welfare use that we see now in the immigrant population may remain with us for some time. This raises troubling questions about the impact of this long-term dependency on the immigrants—and on their U.S.-born children.

NATIONAL ORIGIN PATTERNS

There is huge variation in welfare participation among immigrant groups. For example, about 4.3 per cent of households originating in Germany, 26.8 per cent of households originating in Mexico, and 40.6 per cent of households originating in the former Soviet Union are covered by Medicaid. Similarly, about 17.2 per cent of households originating in Italy, 36 per cent from Mexico and over 50 per cent in the Dominican Republic received some sort of welfare benefit.

A more careful look at these national-origin differentials reveals an interesting pattern: national-origin groups tend to "major" in particular types of benefit. For example, Mexican immigrants are 50 per cent more likely to receive energy assistance than Cuban immigrants. But Cubans are more likely to receive housing benefits than Mexicans.

A Strong Positive Correlation

The SIPP data reveal a very strong positive correlation between the probability that new arrivals belonging to a particular immigrant group receive a particular type of benefit, and the probability that earlier arrivals from the same group received that type of assistance. This correlation remains strong even after we control for the household's demographic background, state of residence, and other factors. And the effect is not small. A 10 percentage point increase in the fraction of the existing immigrant stock who receive benefits from a particular program implies about a 10 per cent increase in the probability that a newly arrived immigrant will receive those benefits.

This confirms anecdotal evidence. Writing in the *New Democrat*—the mouthpiece of the Democratic Leadership Council—Norman Matloff reports that "a popular Chinese-language book sold in Taiwan, Hong Kong, and Chinese bookstores in the United States includes a 36-page guide to SSI and other welfare benefits" and that the "*World Journal*, the largest Chinese-language newspaper in the United States, runs a 'Dear Abby'-style column on immigration matters, with welfare dominating the discussion."

No Refugee/Elderly Welfare Gap

And the argument that the immigrant-native "welfare gap" is caused by refugees and/or elderly immigrants? We can check its validity by removing from the calculations all immigrant households that either originate in countries from which refugees come or that contain any elderly persons.

Result: 17.3 per cent of this narrowly defined immigrant population receives benefits, v. 13 per cent of native households that do not contain any elderly persons. Welfare gap: 4.3 percentage points (proportionately, 33 per cent). The argument that the immigrant welfare problem is caused by refugees and the elderly is factually incorrect.

Conservatives typically stress the costs of maintaining the welfare state. But we must not delude ourselves into thinking that nothing is gained from the provision of antibiotics to sick children or from giving food to poor families.

At the same time, however, these welfare programs introduce a cost which current calculations of the fiscal costs and benefits of immigration do not acknowledge and which might well dwarf the current fiscal expenditures. That cost can be expressed as follows: To what extent does a generous welfare state reduce the work incentives of current immigrants, and change the nature of the immigrant flow by influencing potential immigrants' decisions to come—and to stay?

"The total [government] expenditures on natives per capita are much greater than the expenditures on immigrants per capita."

IMMIGRANTS DO NOT ABUSE THE WELFARE SYSTEM

Part I: Michael Fix, Jeffrey S. Passel, and Wendy Zimmermann; Part II: Julian Simon

In Part I of the following two-part viewpoint, Michael Fix, Jeffrey S. Passel, and Wendy Zimmermann assert that while immigrants participate in welfare programs at a slightly higher rate than native-born Americans, the majority of immigrants on welfare are elderly or refugees. The authors refute George Borjas's argument that immigrants use welfare at a disproportionate rate by asserting that his numbers are inflated due to the inclusion of payments that are not typically considered welfare. In Part II, Julian Simon agrees that welfare payments are slightly higher for immigrants than for natives, but argues that total government expenditures are higher for natives than for immigrants. Fix is the director of the Urban Institute's Immigrant Policy Program. Passel is the director for the Program for Research on Immigration Policy. Zimmermann is a research associate of the Urban Institute in Washington, D.C. Simon is the author of *The Economic Consequences of Immigration*.

As you read, consider the following questions:

1. Why is the CPS data used by the Urban Institute superior to that of the SIPP data used by Borjas, in the authors' opinion?
2. According to Simon, what are the two conclusions that can be drawn from the estimates of government expenditures for immigrants and natives?

Part I: Reprinted from "Summary of Facts About Immigrants' Use of Welfare," by Michael Fix, Jeffrey S. Passel, and Wendy Zimmermann, published by the Urban Institute, Washington, D.C., April 1996, by permission of the publisher (endnote omitted). Part II: Reprinted from "Immigration Exploitation Myths . . . or Reality?" by Julian Simon, *Washington Times*, March 11, 1996, by permission of the author.

I

Questions have arisen recently about the use of welfare and public assistance by immigrants. We lay out here some key facts about immigrants' welfare use and report the similarities and differences in prominently cited research on this issue conducted by the Urban Institute and George Borjas.

KEY FACTS

- Most immigrants (94 percent in 1993 according to the Current Population Survey, CPS) do not use "welfare" as conventionally defined (to include Aid to Families with Dependent Children, AFDC; Supplemental Security Income, SSI; or General Assistance, GA).
- Overall, immigrants have slightly higher welfare use rates than natives (6.6 versus 4.9 percent). But welfare use among immigrants is concentrated among refugees and elderly immigrants who use welfare at rates disproportionate to their numbers. These two groups make up 21 percent of the immigrant population but 40 percent of welfare users. Non-refugee working-age immigrants use welfare at about the same rate as natives.
- Immigrant welfare use and costs have risen slightly relative to natives since 1990—but we believe the rise owes largely to the concentration of the immigrant population in California which has generous welfare programs, is home to many legalizing immigrants, and has been in recession.
- According to administrative data, immigrants are more likely to use SSI—a cash assistance program for the elderly and disabled—than natives. In 1993, elderly immigrants made up 28 percent of the SSI recipients aged 65 and older, but they made up only 9 percent of the total elderly population. Many of these elderly immigrants have not worked enough quarters in covered U.S. occupations to qualify for Social Security, either because they have not been in the United States long enough or because they worked for employers who have not paid Social Security taxes for them.
- The immigrant group with the fastest growth in SSI use is the disabled. Despite recent growth in use, immigrants continue to make up a smaller share of the disabled SSI population than they do of the general population.
- Poor immigrants remain less likely than poor natives to use welfare (16 versus 25 percent). These findings are confirmed by administrative data: a 1995 Food and Nutrition

Service study found that eligible immigrants who legalized under the Immigration Reform and Control Act of 1986 were less likely to receive food stamps than the general population.

INTERPRETING THE FINDINGS

Similar basic findings—In his May 1996 paper on the subject, Borjas states that the "immigrant-native difference in the probability of receiving cash benefits is small (10.8 vs. 7.3 percent)"—the same basic conclusion reached by Urban Institute studies.

Different definitions of "welfare"—Borjas finds large differences between immigrant and native "welfare" use when he uses a measure that includes cash assistance as well as Medicaid, food stamps, energy assistance, housing assistance and WIC (the supplemental food program for women, infants and children)— programs that go beyond those typically considered "welfare." Among non-cash programs he finds small differences in use rates for each program except Medicaid and the reduced price school lunch program (which is not included in the cumulative measure), where he finds larger differences.

Different data sources—The Urban Institute findings are based on an analysis of the 1993 Current Population Survey (CPS) while Borjas combines 1990 to 1993 data from the Survey of Income and Program Participation (SIPP). Each data source has its advantages. Even after Borjas combines different years of the SIPP, the size of his sample is half that of the 1993 CPS and therefore provides less accurate results for relatively small populations, such as immigrants, and for the even smaller population of immigrants who use welfare. The SIPP, however, reinterviews the same family periodically over the course of 32 months, providing a better picture of welfare use than the one-point-in-time analysis of the CPS.

Different units of analysis—The Urban Institute CPS results are based on an analysis of individuals' use of benefits, while Borjas uses a household level analysis. The household analysis is problematic because it attributes to immigrant-headed households use of welfare by natives in their households, such as children. This is a serious concern since 67 percent of immigrant-headed households contain a native-born person and 52 percent contain a native-born child.

Different results using SIPP individual level data—Elaine Sorensen and Nikki Blasberg of the Urban Institute analyzed individual use of welfare with the SIPP and found that immigrant and native use rates for those of all ages are so close that they are not statistically different for any of the cash or non-cash benefit programs except SSI.

When immigrants and their native-born children are considered together, statistically significant differences emerge in the use of Medicaid and housing assistance. Statistically meaningful differences in SSI use disappear, however. This apparently anomalous result occurs because the foreign-born population is composed of a smaller share of children and a larger share of adults than the general population. For this reason, when the native-born children of immigrants are included in the analysis, use rates of child-oriented services such as Medicaid increase. Conversely, use rates of programs directed largely at adults—like SSI—decline.

II

The pro-immigration camp has now come to believe that government expenditures on recent immigrants are greater than expenditures on natives.

A Drop in the Bucket

But this assertion is false—completely false, viciously false. True, expenditures commonly called "welfare" are about $150 per year greater per immigrant than per native, and have always been higher. But the welfare expenditures are only a drop in the bucket of total government social outlays on both groups. The relevant totals are roughly $3,800 for natives, and roughly $2,200 for immigrants. The piddling welfare expenditures on immigrants are a very red herring in policy debate. Let's consider the elements in the graph that tells this story.

Narrow welfare expenditures: From census and federal administrative data Rebecca Clark of the Urban Institute calculated expenditures for immigrants and natives on Aid to Families with Dependent Children (AFDC), food stamps, Supplemental Security Income (SSI) and General Assistance. Foreign-born persons taken altogether have perhaps a 15 percent higher probability of obtaining these goods and services than do natives. From her data, I estimate that federal expenditures average $404 per year per immigrant, while the average native receives $260. These data for the early 1990s are shown at the base of the immigrant and native columns in the graph. The data on these four federal welfare programs do not, however, include most government payments to the elderly, or expenditures for local public schooling.

Payment to the elderly: Social Security and Medicare, by far the most expensive government transfer programs, are paid mainly to natives. This is because immigrants typically arrive when they are young and healthy, and also because older recent immigrants do not qualify for Social Security.

These expenditures are difficult to estimate for immigrants because the payments differ greatly among age groups. Total federal expenditures of $305 billion in 1992 for Social Security and $133 billion for Medicare indicate expenditures per native of $1,305 and $566, respectively. The authoritative 1975 data suggest the average receipt per immigrant who arrived within the past 25 years is less than a fifth of the average expenditure per native—say $261 and $113, respectively, for argument. (Some allowance for the public support of the immigrant aged is embodied in the relatively heavy SSI payments that substitute for Social Security.) In the graph, these programs dwarf welfare programs.

GOVERNMENT EXPENDITURE PER IMMIGRANT AND PER NATIVE: UNITED STATES, EARLY 1990S

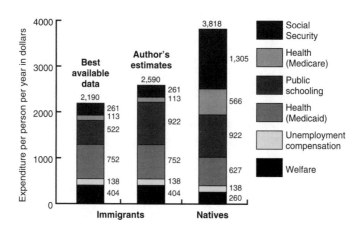

Julian Simon, *Population and Development Review*, March 1996.

Schooling costs: Estimates by Ms. Clark imply $522 per capita for immigrants, and $922 per capita for natives. The expenditures are lower for the immigrant population because the proportion of children among the total immigrant population is smaller than among the total native population. I consider it prudent, however, to assume schooling costs for immigrants equal to those of natives; both estimates are shown in the graph.

Unemployment compensation: Safely assume similar expenditures of

$138 per capita for immigrants and natives, based on earlier solid data.

Medicaid: It is reasonable to assume higher expenditures for immigrants than for natives, because immigrants are somewhat poorer on average than natives. Federal and state Medicaid expenditures are about $90 billion and $70 billion, respectively, so expenditures per person are about $627 for natives, and say perhaps $752 for immigrants.

TOTAL GOVERNMENT EXPENDITURES

Totals: Adding together all the above transfer payments plus schooling costs is the appropriate measure of government expenditures for an assessment of the costs and benefits of immigration. The graph shows the total expenditures on natives per capita are much greater than the expenditures on immigrants per capita—roughly $3,800 vs. $2,200.

It is quite astonishing that the estimates for natives are so much higher than those for immigrants. The gap derives mainly from the costs for the elderly. Of course, these estimates are very messy because of the age composition of the immigrant population—more of whom came in recent years—and other uncertainties in the estimates. But one can draw two conclusions with great surety: (1) The slightly greater expenditures for immigrants on the narrowly defined welfare programs are more than offset by other categories—indeed, dwarfed by them; therefore the welfare programs alone deserve no attention. (2) Overall expenditures for immigrants are not greater than for natives. Rather, expenditures for immigrants are much less than those for natives.

Periodical Bibliography

The following articles have been selected to supplement the diverse views presented in this chapter. Addresses are provided for periodicals not indexed in the *Readers' Guide to Periodical Literature*, the *Alternative Press Index*, the *Social Sciences Index*, or the *Index to Legal Periodicals and Books*.

George J. Borjas — "Know the Flow," *National Review*, April 17, 1995.

Vernon M. Briggs Jr. — "Mass Immigration Worsens Plight of Urban Underclass," *Forum for Applied Research and Public Policy*, Fall 1995.

Daryl R. Buffenstein — "Will New Immigration Barriers Hurt America's Economy? Yes," *Insight*, February 19, 1996. Available from 3600 New York Ave. NE, Washington, DC 20002.

Glenn Garvin — "No Fruits, No Shirts, No Service," *Reason*, April 1995.

Stephen Glass — "Kicked Out," *New Republic*, October 20, 1997.

Nathan Glazer — "The Hard Questions," *New Republic*, December 16, 1996.

Hans-Hermann Hoppe — "Free Immigration or Forced Integration?" *Chronicles*, July 1995. Available from PO Box 800, Mount Morris, IL 61054.

David M. Kennedy — "Can We Still Afford to Be a Nation of Immigrants?" *Atlantic Monthly*, November 1996.

Michael C. Maibach — "Why Our Company Needs Immigrants," *Freeman*, June 1996. Available from the Foundation for Economic Education, Irvington-on-Hudson, NY 10533.

Norman Matloff — "How Immigration Harms Minorities," *Public Interest*, Summer 1996.

Doris M. Meissner — "U.S. Greets Wave of Immigrants, Examines Issues," *Forum for Applied Research and Public Policy*, Fall 1995.

Richard Rayner — "What Immigration Crisis?" *New York Times Magazine*, January 7, 1996.

Murray N. Rothbard — "The Vital Importance of Separation," *Rothbard-Rockwell Report*, April 1994. Available from PO Box 4091, Burlingame, CA 94011.

Robert J. Samuelson   "Immigration and Poverty," *Newsweek*, July 15, 1996.

Julian L. Simon   "Public Expenditures on Immigrants to the United States, Past and Present," *Population and Development Review*, March 1996.

Alan Simpson   "Will New Immigration Barriers Hurt America's Economy? No," *Insight*, February 19, 1996.

Ben J. Wattenberg   "Easy Solution to the Social Security Crisis," *New York Times Magazine*, June 22, 1997.

CHAPTER 3

HOW CAN ILLEGAL IMMIGRATION BE CONTROLLED?

CHAPTER PREFACE

According to records kept by the Immigration and Naturalization Service (INS) and the U.S. Border Patrol, about 300,000 foreigners enter the United States illegally each year. A public outcry by Americans has prompted politicians to develop policies to reduce the number of illegal immigrants.

Until 1997, San Diego, California, was the most popular crossing point for Mexicans trying to enter the United States illegally. Each year, over 300,000 illegal immigrants were arrested by the Border Patrol between 1980 and 1997. In an attempt to reduce the number of illegal border crossings, the INS and Border Patrol instituted Operation Gatekeeper in 1994. Hundreds of extra Border Patrol officers and INS agents were stationed along the 2,000-mile, U.S.-Mexico border, many of them in San Diego County, to apprehend illegal aliens. The effect was almost immediate. A year after Operation Gatekeeper was implemented, arrests of illegal border crossers along the heaviest border crossing area in San Diego decreased by 36 percent, down to 116,015. In 1997, for the first time since 1980, the number of border apprehensions in San Diego County fell below 300,000. Doris Meissner, INS commissioner, announced in October 1997 that the border in San Diego County was virtually under control. The drop in arrests also meant that San Diego fell to fourth place in the number of border apprehensions, behind Tucson, Arizona; McAllen, Texas; and El Centro, California.

Critics of Operation Gatekeeper contend that the program cannot seal the border—it merely forces migrants to shift their crossing points into the more lightly patrolled mountains and deserts east of San Diego. As proof, these critics mention that border apprehensions in eastern San Diego County and in El Centro almost tripled from 1996 to 1997. These figures show, opponents contend, that diverting illegal border crossers to less accessible areas does not necessarily deter them from attempting to enter the United States. Fortifying the border is not the solution to illegal immigration, critics argue, because it does not address the demand for low-wage workers.

Strengthening the U.S. presence along the border, requiring a national identity card, and legislating against illegal immigrants are just some of the responses to illegal immigration that are examined by the authors in the following chapter.

"*We have the power to say 'yes' or 'no' to the oppressive future being planned for us and our progeny.*"

ANTI-ILLEGAL IMMIGRATION LAWS WOULD BENEFIT SOCIETY

James Thornton

Proposition 187 is a 1994 California ballot initiative that would deny public education, health, and social service benefits to illegal immigrants. The measure was under an injunction for three years before a federal judge ruled it was unconstitutional in November 1997. In the following viewpoint, James Thornton, a Roman Catholic priest, argues that Proposition 187 is necessary to protect California from the thousands of illegal immigrants who enter the state daily. Providing public benefits to these illegals is extremely costly, he maintains; Proposition 187 will allow legal residents and citizens to take control of their lives by diminishing the aliens' adverse impact on society and the economy.

As you read, consider the following questions:

1. How many illegal aliens are estimated to cross the U.S.-Mexico border every twenty-four hours, according to the author?
2. Why is it more expensive to teach illegal alien students than English-speaking students, in the author's view?
3. What are the five provisions of Proposition 187, as cited by Thornton?

Reprinted from "SOS in the Golden State," by James Thornton, *New American*, October 31, 1994, by permission of the *New American*.

It is perhaps not fully appreciated by those living outside the Southwest United States how dramatically the area has been transformed since the 1970s—change for the worse, for the most part, and much of it the direct result of unrestricted Third-World immigration and, more specifically, illegal immigration. Nowhere is the change more evident than in California, the "Golden State" as it used to be called with great pride. Bursting with vitality and prosperity only a few years ago, California today is literally overwhelmed with fiscal and social problems: urban decay, rampant crime, declining property values, overcrowding, gang violence, scandalous deficits, "white flight," and rapidly rising expenditures for schools and welfare programs. All of this is combined with a deterioration in services such as libraries, police, and roads, and hosts of associated conditions. And it is no wonder, since every 24 hours an estimated four to five thousand aliens illegally cross the border from Mexico into California. That means that every year from 1.46 to 1.8 million illegals enter the state.

THE CLEAR PICTURE

A cursory glance at the financial picture in California is sufficient to reveal the nature of the difficulties. Approximately 50 percent of all illegal aliens settle in California. Education for these uninvited guests costs the taxpayers of California $3.6 billion per year. And, while money allocated for English-speaking students totals approximately $4,000 per student per year, that for illegal alien students is $6,600 per student per year. The difference has to do with language: Illegal aliens do not speak English and many are illiterate in their own native languages; expensive bilingual programs, mandated by government, drain precious resources needed by citizens.

Health care for illegals in Los Angeles County alone, one of the areas most heavily impacted by the immigration invasion, cost $203.1 million in 1992 and continues to escalate every year. Contributing significantly to this huge financial burden is the fact that three out of four births in publicly funded hospitals in LA are to illegal aliens.

The criminal justice system in Southern California now consumes an inordinate proportion of state and county budgets, LA County, for example, spending approximately $100 million annually. In neighboring Orange County, nearly 60 percent of all homicides are attributable to illegal immigrants and 80 percent of all drug-related crimes are ultimately traced to illegals and foreigners. The annual bill in California for illegal aliens in state prisons is $500 million, which does not include costs of parole and probation. Real expenditures probably exceed $1 billion, and even this is exclusive of the expenses for increased law enforcement, courts, public defenders, etc.

Financial analysts write that the economic downturn in California is not ultimately connected to defense budget cuts and the down-sizing of aerospace industries. The truth, they say, is that taxpayers are moving out of the state in huge numbers, while an underclass hungry for government handouts is moving in. A fundamental structural change is at work, and the lion's share of it is the result of our largely open borders.

Cultural conflict has also become a major cause of dissatisfaction in California. Spurred on by "immigrant rights" groups and by governmental policies that encourage multiculturalism, many recent arrivals from Mexico and Central America are now resisting assimilation; they are intent not only on retaining their old loyalties and folkways, but are attempting to force them on local residents—*reverse* assimilation, in other words. In cities such as Santa Ana, few residents even speak English anymore. Signs and billboards are all in Spanish. American holidays are scorned, yet "Cinco de Mayo" and Mexican Independence Day (September 16th) inspire major celebrations. The Mexican tricolor is ubiquitous, appearing on cars, homes, and stores.

ELECTION FRAUD

Investigators are discovering that many non-citizens are registering and voting in American elections, helped by federal law requiring that ballots be printed in foreign languages to accommodate legal immigrants who become citizens but, paradoxically, do not bother to learn English. Since this helps liberal candidates, attempts by conservative candidates to halt illegal voting bring forth the customary howls about "minority persecution" and "racism." Pro-illegal immigration groups know exactly what they are doing, of course.

In 1990, Latino activists took over the city of Bell Gardens through voter fraud and non-citizen votes. Local residents who complained to authorities about the takeover were, like conservative candidates, pilloried as vicious "racists." The actual seizure of power by people with foreign loyalties in an American city should be an alarm call to patriots, yet it is even more dangerous a development than it may seem at first glance. Radical Mexican nationalist organizations repeatedly vow to "take back" the southwestern states as the seven cities of Aztlan—the name Latino activists give to the southwestern states of the U.S., which, they say, were illegally wrested from Mexico in the 19th century. The Bell Gardens vote, therefore, may be a kind of trial run for the takeover of the whole state and region.

More importantly, activists make no secret of their ultimate intention. In 1993, Los Angeles militant activist Xavier Hermasillo defiantly cried, "We will take you over, house by house, block by block." Perhaps such objectives seem far-fetched and such words preposterous. But if, in a few more decades, those who appreciate our Western heritage no longer constitute a majority in the United States, it may not seem fantastic at all. If present trends continue, immigrants from Latin America—many of them arriving illegally, having no plans to assimilate, and lacking any understanding of the responsibilities of citizenship in a free society—will constitute a majority in the Southwest far sooner than that. How will demands for autonomy or independence be met should American governments remain as spineless as they are now and should present plans to expand the power of the United Nations be fully implemented? Unquestionably, this is an ominous situation.

GRASSROOTS RESPONSE

However, America need not travel that dismal road to disaster. Still constituting a majority, we have the power to say "yes" or "no" to the oppressive future being planned for us and our progeny. California is a perfect case in point. . . . One of the most important pieces of legislation in the history of California [is] Proposition 187—the Save Our State (SOS) initiative. . . . Placed on the ballot in a grassroots voter revolt similar in nature to that which produced the famous Proposition 13 tax measure in 1978, SOS is an example of what American citizens can accomplish if they are sufficiently informed and aroused. . . .

Proposition 187 . . . will accomplish the following:

• Illegal aliens will be forbidden from receiving any public social services whatever and all public social agencies will be required to report to the U.S. Immigration and Naturalization Service (INS) any illegal alien who applies for public benefits. Presently, swayed by false liberal humanitarianism and unduly frightened by radical immigration organizations, local and state government agencies refuse to report illegals to the INS.

• Illegal aliens will be barred from receiving education at the expense of California taxpayers. The law will include elementary and secondary schools as well as higher education. Educational institutions will also be required to report illegal aliens to the INS. There are currently almost 900,000 students in California who are either illegal aliens or the children of illegal aliens.

• Illegal aliens will no longer be eligible for publicly funded health care, except in cases of bona fide emergencies. Public health agencies will be required to report illegal aliens to the INS. "Free" health care is one of the big drawing cards for illegal aliens, who naturally prefer publicly funded agencies and facilities in the U.S. to the inadequate facilities in their home countries. Thus, hundreds of thousands come here for their prenatal and maternity care, and tens of thousands more for cancer therapy, heart surgery, organ transplants, and other high-cost procedures. County and state facilities are inundated by people who are in no way the responsibility of the taxpayers of this country.

AN INCENTIVE TO JOIN THE SYSTEM

The reality is that illegals (at least the adults) have chosen to live outside of the law. Compelling as an illegal's personal plight might be, illegal immigrants are in this country against the wishes of the electorate. Prop. 187 reduces the incentives to reside in California illegally, which resulted in record numbers of resident illegals applying for green cards in 1995, the year after the measure gained approval. It appears that Prop. 187, by altering incentives, can actually induce people to "join the system" and enter mainstream society.

Erick Jackson, *Thinker*, April 30, 1997.

• The manufacture, distribution, sale, or use of false documents by illegal aliens will become a felony, with mandatory fines and imprisonment. Currently, for a few dollars anyone may obtain a false Social Security card, driver's license, resident alien work permit, or any other document that helps illegals establish a kind of shadow legitimacy in the United States. Bogus documents are advertised publicly on the streets of major cities in Southern California and penalties are so nominal that criminals operate virtually with impunity. The situation is not unlike that caused by floods of counterfeit currency in circulation. With forged documents so easily procurable, the integrity of the nation's social structure is gravely at risk. Proponents of the California SOS initiative believe that new penalties will greatly lessen that danger.

• Law enforcement agencies will be required to report criminal illegal aliens to the INS. Furthermore, California's attorney general will be required to report illegal aliens, identified by any state agencies, to the INS. . . . Should California take actions required by the new law, it will then be incumbent on the INS to deport residents who are not in the United States legally. Whether or not the federal government does this will, once again, be the responsibility of an alert citizenry. . . .

CHANGE IN COURSE

Proposition 187 represents a potential turning point for our beloved country. It is proof that a few determined, patriotic citizens can stand up to cowardly politicians and public officials, to special interests, and to the media and education establishments and can actually change the course of history.

The ancients were fond of the motto, *Nulla verba sed acta*—"Not words but deeds." That has, in effect, become the motto of a growing legion of brave citizens in California. Let it now become a motto indelibly inscribed in the hearts of patriotic Americans from coast to coast.

"[*Anti-illegal immigration laws*]
would open the door to greater
discrimination against all those who
'look like immigrants.'"

ANTI-ILLEGAL IMMIGRATION LAWS WOULD HARM SOCIETY

Raúl Hinojosa and Peter Schey

In the following viewpoint, Raúl Hinojosa and Peter Schey contend that faulty reasoning is behind Proposition 187—a ballot initiative that would prohibit undocumented immigrants from receiving public health care, education, and social services. Immigrants—both legal and undocumented—pay taxes to the federal government and use fewer social services than legal U.S. residents, the authors assert. They maintain that anti-illegal immigration laws would force people to become government informants, thus transforming society into a police state. Proposition 187 was ruled unconstitutional by a U.S. district judge in November 1997. Hinojosa is the research director of the North American Integration and Development Center at the University of California at Los Angeles. Schey is executive director of the Center for Human Rights and Constitutional Law in Los Angeles.

As you read, consider the following questions:

1. What do all the studies cited have in common, according to the authors?
2. In the authors' view, what is the main mission of the anti-immigration studies?
3. What are the two possible scenarios if Proposition 187 is implemented, according to Hinojosa and Schey?

Reprinted from "The Faulty Logic of the Anti-Immigration Rhetoric," by Raúl Hinojosa and Peter Schey, *NACLA Report on the Americas*, vol. 29, no. 3, pp. 18–24, by permission. Copyright 1997 by the North American Congress on Latin America, 475 Riverside Dr., #454, New York, NY 10115-0122.

The upsurge of support in California for Proposition 187, the so-called "Save Our State" ballot initiative, is an ominous manifestation of the fear many U.S. voters have of their future position in a rapidly integrating world economy and an increasingly multicultural society. The Californian economy is undergoing radical changes whose origins lie principally in shifting East-West and North-North relations—the end of the Cold War, the new Pacific economy, and the passage of the GATT [General Agreement on Tariffs and Trade]. Californians, however, have been led by politicians to believe that the state's fiscal crisis is rooted in its North-South relations, particularly its long-term dependence on immigrant labor from Mexico and Central America.

The image of Latin American welfare mothers jumping the border to live off taxpayers and to populate the schools with "illegal" non-English speaking children was too politically potent for Governor Wilson's fledgling and floundering re-election campaign to pass up. Wilson used Proposition 187 to energize the Republican Party's political base of older white male conservative voters who are openly anxious about the dwindling white majority in the state.

A FAR-FETCHED CLAIM

The proposition aspires to transport white voters back to manifest destiny: their God-given right to control and purify the Southwest borderlands. To achieve this, proponents of the measure make the far-fetched claim that the denial of essential services to undocumented immigrants will deter new migrants as well as encourage undocumented residents already in the country to leave voluntarily. The formal argument for the ballot initiative states this mission in militaristic language:

> WE CAN STOP ILLEGAL ALIENS. If the citizens and the taxpayers of our state wait for the politicians in Washington and Sacramento to stop the incredible flow of ILLEGAL ALIENS, California will be in economic and social bankruptcy. We have to act and ACT NOW! On our ballot, Proposition 187 will be the first giant stride in ultimately ending the ILLEGAL ALIEN invasion.

As imitation propositions, bills and campaigns begin to spring up across the country, national and local debates must be made to focus on the wildly false and fundamentally racist claims concerning the economic impact of U.S.-Mexican migration, as well as on the disastrous socioeconomic, transnational and human consequences of any attempt to actually implement these misguided policies. Not only do Prop 187 advocates exaggerate the fiscal costs of immigration, but Mexican-U.S. migrant labor is in fact a major subsidy to California, especially for the prototypical pro-187 voter.

FAULTY STUDIES

Prop 187 proponents like to point to a series of studies conducted in the early 1990s which concluded that immigration is a burden on taxpayers and a growing part of the state's fiscal crisis. All of these studies share a similar set of suspect estimating techniques concerning the number of undocumented immigrants, the cost of their use of social services, their tax contributions, and the overall economic benefits of Mexican immigration.

First of all, each of these studies can be faulted for their inflated estimates of the number of undocumented immigrants, undocumented children attending schools, and the percentage of these immigrants who are actually deportable by federal law. In his 1994–95 budget, Governor Wilson, for example, stated that there were 2,083,000 undocumented immigrants in California in 1993, including 456,000 undocumented children between the ages of 5 and 17. Interestingly, the Immigration and Naturalization Service (INS), reputed for its excessively high estimates of the nation's undocumented population, reported only 1,441,000 undocumented immigrants in California in October, 1992. Using this estimate and the methodology of California's Department of Finance, one finds that the Governor overestimates by 111,528 (or 24%) the number of undocumented children attending public schools in California.

Starting with inflated numbers, none of these studies bother to estimate how many of the so-called "illegal aliens" are actually deportable under federal law. U.S. immigration law allows many categories of undocumented people to legalize their status by, for example, obtaining political asylum, amnesty, "adjustment of status" through close family members who are legal residents, and "suspension of deportation" based on seven years of continuous residence in the United States. These categories may represent a significant subset of the undocumented population. As was established during the 1980 Texas school case argued before the Supreme Court, the majority of undocumented children attending public school eventually legalize their immigration status.

One of the more sinister methodological tools used in these studies is the creation of a separate accounting category for "Citizen Children of Undocumented Persons." This sort of blood-lineage accounting is not only contrary to the constitutional definition of what constitutes citizenship rights in the United

States, but also echoes the kind of fiscal accounting that was used in apartheid South Africa to differentiate the rights of particular legal-ethnic categories.

These anti-immigrant studies then move on to their main mission: producing a cost-benefit analysis with high estimates of the cost of providing social services to undocumented immigrants, and low estimates of local tax revenues collected from this sector of the population.

Undocumented Immigrants Pay Taxes

These studies all acknowledge that undocumented immigrants contribute a significant amount in taxes once federal, state and local taxes are added together. California agencies, however, argue that immigrants pay a greater proportion of taxes to the federal government even though local governments are responsible for providing the bulk of social services. What is not mentioned, of course, is that this disproportionate burden upon localities is true for most working-class households in the United States. The real issue is that the federal government has gradually shifted the burden of social-service provision to local governments. Not only is immigration irrelevant to this phenomenon, but according to a 1994 Rand Corporation study, undocumented immigrants actually buffer the effect because they use social services far less than the typical working-class household. This is not surprising given that federal law already renders undocumented immigrants ineligible for most social and health services. Moreover, recent immigrants tend to be healthier than the typical U.S. citizen.

In order to inflate the cost of immigration, Governor Wilson's office added up all current state expenditures (including roads, parks, corporate subsidies, and debt payments), and then calculated the percentage spent on undocumented immigrants and the children of undocumented immigrants based on their share of the population. Notably, if such a formula were used to determine the cost-benefit contribution of all California residents, the gap between what is received from the government and what is contributed in taxes would be wider for U.S. citizens than it is for immigrants. . . .

Two Possible Scenarios

If Proposition 187 is implemented, the result would be one of two possible scenarios, both of which would spell disaster for California. In the first scenario, the proponents of Prop 187 get what they say they want: all undocumented migrants go back to

Mexico and no more come to California. This would be devastating to the Californian economy and the fiscal well-being of the state. Even assuming unrealistic conjectures of the ability of U.S. residents to rapidly fill jobs formerly held by undocumented migrants, the higher wages required by U.S. residents would mean big price hikes for numerous products and a collapse in output not experienced since the Great Depression. This economic crisis would set off a much larger fiscal crisis, making the current state deficit look small by comparison. The real income of all California residents, particularly pro-187 voters, would fall in ways unheard-of in the post–World War II era. In Mexico, real wages—particularly in the poor rural sectors— would suffer the greatest decline, acutely exacerbating social and political tensions.

Was This the Intent?

Did the makers of the proposition really intend for children to not be immunized? Did they think about the increase of communicable diseases in our communities? Did they really intend for persons to bleed to death because they are afraid to come to the emergency room? Did they really mean that no pre-natal care is better for our world? There are no words for the outrage I feel for my sisters and brothers who are treated this way.

Sharon Rhodes-Wickett, *Christian Social Action*, February 1995.

The other possible outcome is that Prop 187 does not deter undocumented immigration and that the undocumented population in California is simply driven deeper underground. Researchers generally agree that this is the more likely scenario since immigrants are not drawn to the United States because of the presumed availability of social services. The employers of undocumented workers, traditionally strong supporters of Governor Wilson, also likely believe this will be the outcome. Otherwise, they would have vocally opposed Prop 187 just as they have opposed efforts to limit their access to undocumented labor in the past.

If the proposition is implemented, wages for undocumented immigrants will probably fall, as they did after weak employer-sanctions provisions went into effect under the Immigration Reform and Control Act (IRCA) in 1986. As wages and working conditions for undocumented workers deteriorate, the demand for their labor will rise.

The optimal scenario for pro-187 voters is that undocumented immigrants continue to come to the United States, work at even lower wages, and do not use any social services. This is, in fact, the policy approach that Pete Wilson advocated in 1986 when, as a state senator, he pushed for special provisions to allow the entry of undocumented workers as part of IRCA. It also explains Governor Wilson's call for a new *bracero* program in a speech at the right-wing Heritage Foundation in Washington immediately after the passage of Prop 187.

A NEGATIVE IMPACT ON SOCIETY

While perhaps a rosy short-term outcome for Governor Wilson's business supporters, the overall long-term impact on Californian society would be negative in a variety of ways. First of all, public health would be seriously compromised. Pregnant women would be denied prenatal care while children who have been abused or neglected would not receive social services. Undocumented residents with serious illnesses would be denied needed medical attention. Others, fearing deportation, would be deterred from seeking medical care when sick. Communicable diseases would spread, endangering the health of all Californians.

Medical experts point out that the cost of health care would skyrocket under Prop 187 since health workers are mandated to provide expensive emergency services that could have been avoided by far less costly early intervention. The Chief of Staff of the Los Angeles County Medical Center, the largest public hospital in California, predicts that while Proposition 187 may save the state about $9 million annually, the costs for emergency care as well as for the treatment of U.S. citizens with communicable diseases will rise by $47 million, resulting in net costs of over $38 million.

Proposition 187 would also bar undocumented children from attending public schools. Testimonials from teachers and educators throughout the country speak of the irreparable harm this would cause these children. Since most undocumented children eventually become lawful permanent residents, and later U.S. citizens, the long-term costs to California of implementing Prop 187 are enormous. These youngsters would become largely unemployable, rely extensively on public-support programs, and be more likely to turn to crime to support themselves.

MOVING TOWARD A POLICE STATE

If implemented, Prop 187 will also move California well along the road towards a police state. The measure mandates a vast state network of informants. Employees of schools, medical clinics, social-service agencies, and state and local law-enforcement agencies would all be required to ferret out suspected undocumented residents and report them to the INS and the Justice Department. Of course, none of these people have the training to make such determinations. This would open the door to greater discrimination against all those who "look like immigrants."

"Illegal aliens are here for jobs. . . . So the only effective way to deter illegal immigration must include the worksite."

A NATIONAL IDENTIFICATION SYSTEM WOULD REDUCE ILLEGAL IMMIGRATION

Susan Martin

Susan Martin is the executive director of the U.S. Commission on Immigration Reform, a bipartisan congressional commission established to study U.S. immigration policy. In the following viewpoint, Martin argues that establishing a computerized registry using the Social Security numbers of all residents eligible to work in the United States would deter illegal immigrants from obtaining jobs in the United States. She maintains that a computerized registry would reduce the potential for discrimination by requiring everyone who is starting a new job to present the same documentation. It would also reduce the potential of employers accepting fraudulent documents, Martin contends, and the amount of time and paperwork needed by employers to verify the legitimacy of their employees.

As you read, consider the following questions:

1. What measures does Martin propose to protect the civil liberties of those who use a computerized registry for employment verification?
2. What action does the author recommend to ensure that the rights of individual workers are not threatened by errors in the system?
3. How can the number of fraudulent documents be reduced, in Martin's opinion?

Reprinted from Susan Martin's testimony before the U.S. Senate Committee on the Judiciary, Subcommittee on Immigration and Claims, March 14, 1995.

In our first report to Congress in 1994, *U.S. Immigration Policy: Restoring Credibility*, the Commission sought to recommend a comprehensive strategy. We chose to focus much of that report on measures to control illegal immigration, because growing frustration about it undermines our first commitment to legal immigration in the national interest. . . .

Let me sum up the Commission's reasons for proposing that we develop a better system for worksite verification. Reducing the employment magnet is the linchpin of a comprehensive strategy to reduce illegal immigration. Illegal aliens are here for jobs. That is the attraction. So the only effective way to deter illegal immigration must include the worksite.

Better border enforcement is necessary, but not sufficient. Visa overstayers make up fully one-half of the influx of illegal aliens, 150,000 out of 300,000 who take up permanent residence here illegally every year, on top of an illegal population that exceeds 4 million already. No amount of border enforcement can solve that half of the problem—the people who enter legally and then do not leave when they should.

We simply must develop a better system for verifying work authorization. That is central to effective enforcement of employer sanctions.

The system we have now, the I-9 process, is doubly flawed. It does not do what it was supposed to do, namely deter the employment of illegal aliens. What it does do, we do not want—namely, burden businesses with paperwork, while creating abundant opportunities for fraud and forgeries. It may even provide an excuse for, if it does not actually provoke, discrimination against workers who happen to look or sound foreign.

Honest employers are caught between the proverbial rock and a hard place. Because the system is based on documents, employers are placed in a position of making judgments many do not feel qualified to make.

Identifying forgeries is difficult, even for trained professionals. If an employer accepts false documents presented by an unauthorized worker, that employer is vulnerable to employer sanctions for having hired someone under false pretenses, regardless of the fact that they may well have been fooled themselves. Yet, if an employer chooses to doubt particular documents and asks for more from some workers and not from others, that is discrimination.

THE MOST PROMISING OPTION

The Commission believes that we must develop a better system of worksite verification and that the way to do it is through pilot testing. After examining a wide range of alternatives, the Commission concluded that the most promising option for secure, nondiscriminatory verification is a computerized registry based on the social security number.

For decades, all workers have been required to provide employers with their social security number. Depending on the results of pilot projects that are now being designed, the cumbersome I-9 process, with its dozens of documents and blizzard of paper, could be replaced by a single electronic step to validate information every worker must already provide.

The Commission examined the Telephone Verification System, called TVS, which the INS [Immigration and Naturalization Service] has been testing. We are aware that the INS will expand this system, first from 9 to 200 sites, and eventually to 1,000 sites. We support this INS effort—but only as an interim measure. It is not the solution.

The fatal flaw in the TVS system is that it ultimately depends on self-attestation. Workers are asked whether they are citizens or aliens. It is simply not sound law enforcement to rely on lawbreakers to tell the truth.

The Commission also looked at the feasibility and effectiveness of reducing the number of documents used in verification. Again, we support such efforts as interim measures. But the fatal flaw here is the vulnerability of all documents to counterfeiting. We heard expert testimony that any document, even the most tamper-proof ones, can be forged so well that only experts can identify the fakes. Employers cannot be expected to identify counterfeit documents.

WHAT A COMPUTERIZED REGISTRY WILL ACCOMPLISH

The Commission believes electronic validation of the social security number is the most promising option because it holds great potential for accomplishing the following:

- *Reduction in the potential for fraud.* Using a computerized registry, rather than relying on documents, guards against counterfeits;
- *Reduction in the potential for discrimination.* All workers must present the same information to be validated;
- *Reduction in the time, resources, and paperwork spent by employers in complying with IRCA [Immigration Reform and Control Act of 1986].* INS employees who now chase paper could be redirected to chase down those who knowingly hire illegal workers.

The Commission did not try to micromanage implementation of this recommendation in advance. We deliberately did not spell out precisely how the software of the registry would be designed, although we did specify that just six pieces of information seem necessary: name; social security number; place and date of birth; mother's maiden name; and status code. Nor did we limit the innovation that might be applied in pilot projects to test the registry. But we did speak to some of the most important aspects.

First, focus on those areas with the largest numbers of illegal aliens. The Commission recommends that pilot projects be undertaken in the five high-impact states—California, Texas, Florida, New York, and Illinois. We also recommend that, in time, the pilots should be extended to several less-affected states. But we did not recommend that the registry be tested throughout all of the five states immediately, nor even in all of any one of the states. Pilot projects should start small. Before going to the next phase, we should have results to guide us. . . .

PROTECTIVE MEASURES

The features of pilot programs should include:

• *A means by which employers will access the verification system to validate the accuracy of information given by workers.* We received conflicting testimony about the best way to ascertain that a new hire is who he or she claims to be. Some believe that the tamper-resistant driver's licenses now being issued by many states can do the job; others strongly advocate testing a more secure social security card.

But it is also possible that electronic validation through a telephone system would require no document at all. Every ATM system uses a PIN number to protect our money. We should test to see if personal information, such as the mother's maiden name and date of birth, that is already part of the social security database, can serve the same function for worksite verification.

• *Measures to ensure the accuracy of the necessary data.* Improvements must be made in both the INS and Social Security Administration databases to ensure that employers have timely and reliable access to what they need. Frankly, no one can be opposed to improving the reliability of the data in these agencies. There is no protection of liberty in government error.

• *Measures to ensure against discrimination.* One key to the Commission's recommendation is that employers would no longer have to ascertain whether a worker is a citizen or an alien, native-born or an immigrant. All workers would have to present the same information to be validated.

• *Measures to protect civil liberties.* Explicit protections should be devised to ensure that the registry is used only for its intended purposes. The Commission believes that electronically validating the social security number could be used to ascertain eligibility for public benefits without damage to civil liberties, because everyone receiving public assistance must already present a social security number, just as they do for work. But the registry is not to be used for routine identification purposes, and there must be penalties for inappropriate use of the verification process. The Commission's unanimous, unequivocal view is that no one should be required to carry a document and produce it on demand to prove their right to be here.

AN ELECTRONIC VERIFICATION SYSTEM IS NEEDED

Better enforcement of the prohibition of employing illegal immigrants is needed. As uncomfortable as the proposition is to many Americans, some system for electronically verifying a person's eligibility to work is needed if employer sanctions are to work, and illegal immigration brought under control.

Mark Krikorian, *San Diego Union-Tribune*, February 16, 1995.

• *Measures to protect privacy.* Explicit provisions must also be built into the system to safeguard individual privacy. The information contained in the registry will be minimal, given its limited purpose. But the Commission is aware that, while access to any one piece of information may not be intrusive, in combination with other information it can lead to privacy violations.

• *Estimates of the start-up time and financial and other costs.* The Social Security Administration made preliminary estimates for the Commission of its cost for pilot projects: $4 million over the first two years for design and development; and annual costs of maintenance and operation of $32 million. Discrepancies referred to the Social Security Administration were estimated to cost $122 million initially and $30 million per year thereafter. So the total cost of the registry over five years, according to the Social Security Administration, would be approximately $300 million.

By way of comparison, the Urban Institute estimates that illegal aliens cost seven states more than $2.1 billion a year. Spending $300 million over five years to save $2 billion each year is a sound investment.

But the INS cost must be added to the SSA [Social Security Administration] estimate. The Clinton Administration's latest budget request calls for $28.3 million for verification system pilots, although this also includes the expanded TVS program. The bulk of the INS cost, however, will be cleaning up their own data, which should be done regardless of the pilot projects to improve worksite verification.

THE COMMISSION'S RECOMMENDATION TO CORRECT ERRORS

• *Specification of the rights, responsibilities, and impact on individual workers and employers.* In particular, the Commission recommendation for false negatives is that no one—no one—should be fired if their employer does not get a validation code from the registry after hiring. It is entirely possible that a new hire has merely given their social security number wrong. There is no one who has a greater incentive to correct errors, whether they are at the INS or the Social Security Administration, than a legitimate worker who has just learned from the registry that there is a problem. Speaking as someone who pays into the social security system, I want to be sure that the number I have been using is correct—and has not been misappropriated by an illegal alien.

• *A plan for phasing in the system.* Pilot projects should test various methods for phasing in improvements in worksite verification, according to the test results.

An evaluation of pilot program results with these criteria must include objective measures and procedures to determine whether current problems related to fraud, discrimination, and excessive paperwork requirements for employers are effectively overcome, without imposing undue costs on the government, employers, or employees. The evaluation should pay particular attention to the effectiveness of the measures used to protect civil liberties and privacy.

HOW TO REDUCE FRAUDULENT DOCUMENTS

The Commission also recommends reducing the fraudulent access to so-called "breeder documents," particularly birth certificates, that can be used to establish an identity in this country. We recommend these steps:

- A standardized application form for birth certificates;
- Interstate and intrastate matching of birth and death records;
- Only certified copies of birth certificates issued by states should be accepted by federal agencies;
- Standard design and paperstock for all certified copies of birth certificates to reduce counterfeiting;
- Encouraging states to computerize birth records depositories.

The Commission further recommends imposition of greater penalties on those producing or selling fraudulent documents. RICO [Racketeer Influenced and Corrupt Organizations (Act)] provisions to facilitate racketeering investigations also should cover conspiracy to produce and sell fraudulent documents.

Those are the Commission's recommendations on worksite verification.

INTERIM STEPS

Let me add one more note about worksite enforcement. While improved verification is essential, there are interim steps that can be taken to reduce the magnet that jobs present for illegal aliens. The Commission recommends:

- Enhanced resources for investigation of labor standards violations;
- Greater coordination between the Department of Labor and INS in enforcement of employer sanctions and labor standards;
- More targeted enforcement of employer sanctions on industries with a history of illegal alien labor; and
- More proactive enforcement of antidiscrimination laws.

Together, these and other strategies recommended by the Commission should help make jobs attractive to U.S. workers, while identifying and penalizing employers who knowingly hire illegal aliens.

|"*A national identification system*
|*[is] an ill-conceived idea that would*
|*. . . fail to halt illegal immigration.*"

A NATIONAL IDENTIFICATION SYSTEM WOULD NOT REDUCE ILLEGAL IMMIGRATION

John J. Miller and Stephen Moore

In the following viewpoint, John J. Miller and Stephen Moore argue that a computerized national registry of Social Security numbers to verify a worker's legal status is a dangerous intrusion into a person's right to privacy that will do little to reduce illegal immigration. Many employers who hire illegal aliens are aware that their workers are undocumented, the authors contend. Furthermore, they assert, it would be easy to create fraudulent documents to fool employers who try to be law-abiding. Miller is vice president of the Center for Equal Opportunity, a Washington, D.C.-based think tank. Moore is the director of fiscal policy studies at the Cato Institute in Washington, D.C.

As you read, consider the following questions:

1. According to the Bureau of the Census, how many illegal aliens are living in the United States, as cited by the authors?
2. How would a national computerized registry affect hiring decisions between employers and job applicants, in the authors' opinion?
3. According to Miller and Moore, what measures would reduce illegal immigration?

Reprinted from "A National ID System: Big Brother's Solution to Illegal Immigration," by John J. Miller and Stephen Moore, *Cato Policy Analysis*, September 7, 1995, by permission of the Cato Institute, Washington, D.C.

Illegal immigration has become one of the key political issues of the 1990s, especially in border states such as California. Because an estimated 4 million illegal aliens are living in the United States today, a growing number of Americans are demanding tough measures from the federal government to deter illegal entry. In response, federal policymakers are now considering the creation of a national identification system—an ill-conceived idea that would grant the government vast new police-state powers, require citizens to surrender basic freedoms and privacy rights, and fail to halt illegal immigration.

Almost all of the major immigration "reform" measures now being debated would establish some sort of federal worker registry. A computerized database would contain information on every citizen and permanent legal resident of the United States. Before a business could enter a private contractual arrangement to hire a worker, it essentially would have to ask for the federal government's permission. The employer would try to verify a prospective employee's Social Security number against the newly established national database. If the computer registry failed to recognize the Social Security number as valid, the government would forbid the employer to hire the worker. The plan would cover all workers, including native-born citizens, and probably require national identification cards with biometric indicators such as photographs, fingerprints, and possibly even retina scans for all 130 million Americans in the labor force.

The leaders of virtually every libertarian, conservative, and civil liberties organization in America have denounced the computer registry as "misguided and dangerous.". . .

The computer registry will impose large costs on American citizens—in terms of both dollars and lost liberties. American workers will pay a high price for a system that will have at best a negligible effect on deterring unlawful entries into the United States. In the hysteria over illegal immigration, some policymakers in Washington have forgotten that America is a free and open society. Some level of illegal immigration is the price we pay for our freedoms and liberties. Congress may want to trade off Americans' basic rights in order to combat illegal immigration, but the public should not.

THE FAILED LEGACY OF EMPLOYER SANCTIONS

Most illegal immigrants come to the United States in search of employment, not to go on welfare. For many years federal officials have attempted to deter illegal immigration by denying undocumented aliens access to the U.S. job market. In 1986 Congress passed the "employer sanctions" provision of the Immigration Reform and Control Act. Employer sanctions made it a crime for employers to knowingly hire illegal aliens. Under IRCA, job applicants must prove either their citizenship or their legal residence by completing an I-9 Form before they can begin work. Business owners who fail to comply with the law and knowingly hire illegal immigrants can face thousands of dollars in fines and, in the severest cases, prison sentences.

After a decade of experience with employer sanctions, any objective assessment could only conclude that the law has been an unmitigated failure. Employer sanctions have done virtually nothing to halt illegal immigration. The number of illegal immigrants apprehended at the Mexican border rose steadily from 1989 through 1993 (see Figure 1). In 1994, 10 years after employer sanctions were established, 1 million illegal immigrants were apprehended. That is not altogether surprising. Before passage of IRCA, a General Accounting Office study reported that employer sanctions had been unsuccessful in virtually every developed country that had tried them.

Despite the failure of employer sanctions, much of the hysteria over illegal immigration is not confirmed by the official statistics on the size of the illegal alien population. The Bureau of the Census estimates that there are now 4 million illegal aliens living in the United States and that about 300,000 more settle permanently each year. Four million illegal immigrants is undeniably a large number of people, but it is far below the "invading army" of 8 million to 10 million aliens regularly reported in the media and by anti-immigrant lobbyists. Illegal aliens constitute only about 1.5 percent of the 260 million people living in the United States. Surely that number does not require draconian enforcement measures that would touch every single American worker and employer—especially the majority of Americans who do not live in areas with large numbers of illegal aliens. . . .

THE NATIONAL COMPUTER REGISTRY PROPOSAL

Instead of rethinking the failed strategy of enforcing immigration law at the workplace by turning employers into INS cops, many policymakers have called for even more draconian measures. The U.S. Commission on Immigration Reform, chaired by former Texas representative Barbara Jordan, conceded that employer sanctions had failed to deter illegal immigration. The commission announced in 1994 that current methods of worker verification were "too susceptible to fraud, particularly through counterfeiting of documents . . . [and contribute to] discrimination against foreign-looking and foreign-sounding workers." But the commission went on to endorse "a simpler, more fraud-resistant system for verifying work authorization."

FIGURE 1: IMPACT OF EMPLOYER SANCTIONS ON APPREHENSIONS AT THE MEXICAN BORDER

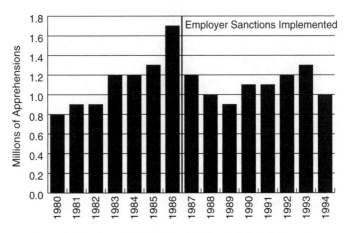

Source: Immigration and Naturalization Service, Statistical Division.

John J. Miller and Stephen Moore, *A National ID System*, September 7, 1995.

In fact, what the commission has proposed is anything but simple. Hiring decisions are currently private contractual arrangements between employers and job applicants. The employer offers a job, the applicant accepts, and work can begin almost immediately. Under the commission's proposed plan, employers would have to verify the Social Security numbers of employees by matching them against a national worker registry maintained by a new federal bureaucracy. The registry would then verify the Social Security number in question and either permit or forbid every individual decision to hire. In other words, the government would, for the first time in history, require employers to submit all of their hiring decisions for approval to a federal bureaucrat.

Most advocates of a computer registry system acknowledge that it could work only in conjunction with a national ID card. Without a national identifier, neither the government nor the employer would have any way of verifying that the person presenting a Social Security number was the actual holder of that number. Illegal aliens could easily use other people's Social Security cards. Senator Dianne Feinstein has even suggested an identification card with "a magnetic strip on which the bearer's unique voice, retina pattern, or fingerprint is digitally encoded."

Senator Alan Simpson has consistently argued that for employer sanctions to work effectively, an ID card is necessary. In the 1990 Immigration Act, he sought an experimental card with a biometric component, such as a fingerprint, and a Social Security number. More recently, in Senate hearings on May 10, 1995, Simpson reaffirmed the necessity of an ID card. "A [worker] verification system must have two functions. It must verify that a name corresponds to someone who is authorized to work. And then verifying the identity, that the person claiming the name and the number is not an imposter. The use of a biometric identifier, such as a fingerprint, is needed if this function is to perform reliably.". . .

THE COMPUTER REGISTRY AND PRIVACY

The Jordan commission [U.S. Commission on Immigration Reform] maintains that a national ID system could be implemented without invading Americans' privacy rights. The commission insists that the computer registry and the ID card would never be used for purposes other than employment verification. Those assurances are less than convincing. The history of government programs indicates that privacy rights are violated routinely whenever expediency dictates that government information be used for expanded purposes.

Consider, for instance, the expanding role of the Social Security card in our society. Created in 1935, its sole purpose was to facilitate the Social Security system. Individuals were assigned numbers so that the proper governing authority could easily account for contributions made to the Social Security fund. Nonetheless, the use of the numbers grew steadily over the years. Starting in 1961 the Civil Service Commission began using Social Security numbers to identify all federal employees. In 1962 the Internal Revenue Service started requiring taxpayers' Social Security numbers to appear on all completed tax returns. The SSA disclosed Social Security numbers to the private sector until public outrage halted the practice in 1989. The disclosures affected more than 3 million Americans.

The computer revolution made use of Social Security numbers prevalent in myriad everyday private and public transactions. Everything from credit to employment to insurance to many states' driver's licenses requires a Social Security number.

Social Security numbers have become de facto national identifiers. All that from a number whose original purpose was to do nothing more than track the amount of money paid into the Social Security system. . . .

The potential for abuse of a national ID system is greater than it has been of any previous government program. The personal information stored in a national worker registry would have to be widely available to the public—more than 6 million employers, after all, would need access to it. Many private companies would have motives for tapping into the information stored in a national worker registry. Market research firms routinely compile information from public records, such as mortgage rolls, that they use to estimate annual income and other characteristics to create a consumer profile. They also pay top dollar for information kept by the federal government. With increasing frequency, government agencies are becoming eager sellers. According to *Business Week*, "The government is actively selling huge amounts of personal information to listmakers." One "information broker" recently told the *Wall Street Journal*, "Everything is available for a price." According to a 1993 poll, 53 percent of Americans oppose a national identity card system because "it would give the federal government too much control over all Americans.". . .

A COMPUTER REGISTRY WILL NOT REDUCE ILLEGAL IMMIGRATION

Many members of Congress and ordinary American citizens may believe that even $3 billion to $6 billion is a small price to pay to reduce illegal immigration. Yet that hugely expensive program will fail to substantially deter illegal immigration.

One factor that will foil the worker registry is the erroneous assumption that employers who hire illegal immigrants do so unwittingly. Many businesses and households that employ an illegal alien know full well that the worker is undocumented. They will continue that behavior, whether or not the federal government chooses to track the entire workforce with a national worker registry.

As the experience with employer sanctions has shown, honest employers who want to play by the rules in running their businesses will face a hefty new burden imposed by Washington. Those who want to skirt the law will pay workers cash or accept forged documents. Says a director of the Amalgamated Clothing and Textile Workers Union in New York, "If a guy running a sewing loft or a laundry or a restaurant needs to cut labor costs, he knows he can hire a few illegal workers, pay them less than the minimum wage, and get away with it." For those employers, sanctions have been irrelevant. The first felony indictment under the employer sanctions law did not come down until August 1994—eight years after employer sanctions were first adopted. The job magnet that attracts illegal immigrants will maintain its strong pull. The . . . problem is one of demand, not supply.

Moreover, no government ID card is fraud resistant for long—unless we move toward a 1984-style system with computer microchips, fingerprints, retina scans, and the like. Employer sanctions and I-9 Forms have given rise to a cottage industry in fake identification. There is no reason to believe that black-market entrepreneurs will abandon a lucrative business just because the federal government thinks it is getting clever. Phony worker documents are available for as little as $30 today in cities with large immigrant populations. The best a worker registry can hope to accomplish is to push up those costs temporarily as forgers update their techniques.

HOW TO REDUCE ILLEGAL IMMIGRATION

If America hopes to compete and win in today's global economy, policymakers need to realize that the importation of human capital is one of America's greatest competitive advantages. U.S. immigration policy should focus on attracting newcomers who will make productive contributions to our economy and society and on keeping out those who would become public charges or engage in criminal activities. U.S. policy should also be formulated within the promising larger framework, begun with the North American Free Trade Agreement, for liberating and integrating the economies of the Western Hemisphere. The following steps would be consistent with that approach:

• Increase legal immigration quotas. One of the most effective ways of deterring illegal immigration is to allow more people to come through lawful channels. As a share of the population, immigrants today are far below historical levels for the United States.

The overriding economic impact of immigrants is to raise the standard of living of American citizens. Immigrants are economically advantageous to the United States for several reasons: 1) they are self-selected on the basis of motivation, risk-taking, dedication to the work ethic, and other attributes that are beneficial to a nation; 2) they tend to come to the United States when they are in their prime working years; 3) they start new businesses at a high rate; and 4) because they come to the United States when they are young, they make huge net contributions to old age entitlement programs, primarily Social Security.

• Experiment with a guest worker program. Many illegal immigrants have no intention of settling permanently in the United States. They are sojourners who want to work hard, earn a good wage, and then return home. America has experimented with guest worker programs in the past. Economist Julian Simon has shown that when the bracero program was in effect in the 1950s, illegal immigration declined to a trickle.

• Promote economic growth in the Americas by creating a hemispheric free-trade zone. Expanding free trade in Latin America will create jobs and prosperity for Mexicans and other neighbors, thus reducing the economic and political instability that generates mass migration to the United States. Congress should complete Ronald Reagan's vision of a hemispheric free-trade zone. As nations grow richer through free trade, the natural movement of people across national borders will become less and less of a political problem. The bipartisan Commission for the Study of International Migration and Cooperative Economic Development made that point in its 1990 report to Congress, arguing that "expanded trade between the sending countries and the United States is the single most important long-term remedy to the problem" of illegal immigration.

• Restrict welfare eligibility of legal and illegal immigrants. Many Americans' current hostility toward immigration is tied to the concern that immigrants abuse America's welfare programs. Although the evidence suggests that that is not true of most newcomers—whether legal or illegal—it may be true of some. Immigrants should be denied all public assistance benefits, except for emergency medical care, for at least their first five years in the United States. . . . That would be consistent with a policy of immigration yes, welfare no. There would be no shortage of hard-working immigrants willing to come to the United States under those conditions.

• Facilitate the deportation of criminal aliens. America wants to attract law-abiding immigrants who come to contribute to society. Steps should be taken to deport aliens who commit felonies.

• Repeal the employer sanctions law. Since employer sanction laws have had no deterrent effect, they are nothing but a charade. Yet they do substantial harm to legal foreign-born workers in the United States, who have become a suspect class. Congress should never have passed a law that turns employers into immigration cops. Now is the time to fix that mistake.

• Improve border enforcement. The Border Patrol has made significant gains in stopping illegal entries over the last two years, especially in El Paso and San Diego. Those successful experiments need to be made permanent. They should also be expanded to other popular points of entry, such as Nogales, Arizona.

• Tighten visa control. Roughly half of all illegal immigrants enter the United States with legal visas. They become illegal only when their visas expire. Many will eventually return to their homelands and again petition for entry into the United States. If INS and Customs officials kept track of when visa holders left the country, they could deny entry to people who had violated the terms of their visas in the past.

A BAD LAW

It is an iron rule of politics that whenever there is a perceived "crisis" in Washington, Congress responds by passing bad laws. Those laws invariably expand the powers of government. That is a very real danger in the area of immigration reform, especially since a national ID system has implications that range far beyond today's debate over illegal immigration.

The worker registry system recommended by the Commission on Immigration Reform has no redeeming feature: it would be an invasion of basic civil liberties; it would put in place a technology that could be easily expanded for other purposes; it would increase discrimination against Latino and Asian populations; it would carry a price tag in the billions of dollars; it would be fraught with errors and fraud; and, most important, it would not deter illegal immigration. At a time when Americans are loudly demanding more freedom and smaller government, a computer registry is a giant step in the wrong direction.

"The United States . . . must . . .
[deploy] our military to inhibit a
massive influx into the country."

THE UNITED STATES SHOULD MILITARIZE THE U.S.-MEXICO BORDER

Ben J. Seeley

In the following viewpoint, Ben J. Seeley argues in support of the use of the U.S. military to help keep illegal aliens from crossing the U.S.-Mexico border at San Diego. Using the military to patrol the border frees up Border Patrol agents and immigration officials who are needed for interdiction and interior enforcement, he asserts. Seeley contends that the military should be used wherever it would do the most good. Seeley is the executive director of the Border Solution Task Force in San Diego, an organization dedicated to the eradication of illegal immigration.

As you read, consider the following questions:

1. Why does Seeley think that the Mexican government is hypocritical in its reaction to the use of the military to guard the U.S.-Mexico border?
2. How have fences along the San Diego–Tijuana border affected illegal border crossers and the Border Patrol, according to the author?
3. In Seeley's opinion, what factor could precipitate a large migration into the United States?

Reprinted from "Military Plays Vital Role on U.S.-Mexico Border," by Ben J. Seeley, *North County Times* (San Diego, Calif.), September 7, 1997, by permission of the author.

There is a tragic irony that even the suggestion of a more prominent role by our military to combat illegal immigration and smuggling activities sets off a seismic reaction within the confines of certain special interests and hidden-agenda organizations.

In tandem, these groups quickly move to mischaracterize the use of our military to protect our citizens and our borders as Draconian in nature.

Nations that are a prime source of immigrants—for instance, Mexico—fire up every mode of their media to castigate the United States whenever it even considers such an act, yet Mexico has no problem placing troops on its southern borders to halt immigration from South and Central America.

Well-funded, self-serving immigration and civil liberty lawyers join hands with equally well-funded, migrant-rights groups to misstate the constitutional legality of utilizing U.S. troops to halt illegal immigration by falsely interpreting the terms in the Treaty of Guadalupe Hidalgo (1848) as their legal authority.

Meanwhile, tax-supported and well-funded educational and charitable organizations jump on the bandwagon with opportunistic U.S. business interests who love lower U.S. wage rates, to capitalize on the plight of the uprooted migrant and the seemingly helpless U.S. taxpayers.

PROTECTING THE BORDER

In 1988, when first exploring the border separating Tijuana from San Diego, I was astounded by the lack of a distinguishable border fence compounded by the badly maintained patrol-access roads and virtually no lighting. There was a very noticeable absence of law enforcement to combat the illegal carnage and violence in the border region.

With a newfound resolve, thanks to a public outcry, and with the assistance of our military, lights went up, roads were greatly improved and the heavy-duty steel fence was put in place.

These improvements have virtually ended the 300 or more dangerous cross-border, high-speed "drive-throughs" that occurred on a monthly basis.

U.S. taxpayers are no longer forced to spend more than $200,000 per year just for replacing windshields on our patrol vehicles caused by the criminal rock throwers.

The dozens of robberies, rapes and murders of illegal aliens by the border bandits on a monthly basis also came to a halt.

The horrible and tragic deaths of illegal aliens that occurred when they dashed across our busy freeways has almost been eliminated and the drownings due to their trying to cross the swollen, rain-filled rivers is no longer a major problem in the San Diego sector.

These improvements were accomplished by using our military smartly, and the military is continuing to provide more assistance with personnel and surveillance equipment on land, on sea and in the air.

EXTRA EYES AND EARS

Maureen Bossch, a spokeswoman for Joint Task Force 6, the El Paso-based military unit that conducts the border operations, said the military forces were "extra eyes and ears" for domestic Federal agents and typically act as camouflaged observers. While not allowed to make arrests, they have carried out hundreds of observation sorties along the border, passing on information to the United States Border Patrol and drug-enforcement agents. . . .

Ms. Bossch said contact of any kind between armed marines and [civilians] would be highly unusual.

"They're certainly not looking for confrontation with anyone," she said, "whether civilians or drug traffickers."

Sam Howe Verhovek, New York Times, June 29, 1997.

The ports of entry have been complemented with military personnel, which is allowing the customs and the Immigration and Naturalization Service inspectors more time to perform their inspection tasks.

With the aid of military construction, the new triple fence and bollard barrier fence is well under way and, when finished, should help to free up INS and Border Patrol agents for badly needed interior enforcement.

Without an effective interior illegal immigration enforcement program, the border and inland check points are sure to remain over-burdened, and employer sanctions enforcement of the Immigration Reform and Control Act will never be effective in cutting down the pull of the jobs magnet.

THE COLONIAS

An ominous situation has surfaced with regard to the buildup of large colonias [settlements] only a few yards from the border. For instance, El Nido Aguilas colonia, located less than a mile from the Otay Mesa port of entry, is now occupied by about 40,000 migrants.

Only a few hundred yards south of the border and just west of downtown Tijuana lies a more recent development called La Colonia Verde, which is an unplanned community squeezing in about 25,000 people.

In both instances, these *colonias* have no planned infrastructure and, as a consequence, depend on Tijuana for delivery of their water by truck.

An alarm was recently published in the Mexican news media cautioning that a severe water shortage is expected to hit the Tijuana area in just a few years.

This could be catastrophic and should be of major concern to the government administrations on both sides of the border.

The large populations of dislocated migrants residing right on the border are more likely than not to cross over into the United States if water becomes a severe problem.

Therefore, the United States must expedite contingency planning with regard to deploying our military to inhibit a massive influx into the country and to provide humanitarian assistance whenever possible.

An undesirable situation exists along another part of the San Diego sector, and it would be a mistake not to focus some attention on the disruption and chaos illegal drug trafficking and immigration is creating for folks in the more rural eastern part of San Diego County.

These rural areas are desperately short of minimal police protection as well as Border Patrol presence and are being overrun by criminal activities. The military options should be seriously considered if it cannot be brought under control.

While it is clear that the U.S. Border Patrol is the most qualified and best trained to carry out border security and illegal alien-smuggling interdiction and enforcement, there is little doubt that it is understaffed, underfunded and undersupported by our national leaders.

Time is not on our side. Until a commitment is made at the highest levels of our government to allow the INS to seriously deal with the illegal immigration and drug-smuggling problems, we should use our military wherever and whenever it can do the most good.

"[The killing of a Hispanic student by four U.S. Marines] is the result of the . . . militarization of the southern border regions."

THE UNITED STATES SHOULD NOT MILITARIZE THE U.S.-MEXICO BORDER

Revolutionary Worker

The following viewpoint appeared in *Revolutionary Worker*, a publication of the Revolutionary Communist Party. In it, the author contends that militarizing the U.S.-Mexico border is a threat to the safety and security of American residents who live in border towns and to Mexicans who try to cross the border illegally. U.S. troops have shot at and killed Americans and Mexicans; such actions are not mistaken or accidental, *Revolutionary Worker* asserts, but a criminal policy formulated at the highest levels of government.

As you read, consider the following questions:

1. What is the official explanation for the deployment of troops at the border, as cited by *Revolutionary Worker*?
2. What does the military's rules of engagement permit, according to the paper?
3. In the paper's view, what is suspicious about the marines' story in the killing of Esequiel Hernandez?

Reprinted from "The Killers of Joint Task Force 6," *Revolutionary Worker*, July 27, 1997, by permission of RCP Publications, Chicago, Illinois. Subheadings, inserted quotation, and new title have been added by Greenhaven Press.

For Esequiel Hernandez Jr., the afternoon of May 20, 1997, began with the usual after-school routine. After classes let out at Presidio High, Esequiel walked back to his family's cinderblock house in Redford, a small West Texas town on the border with Mexico. He ate a snack and did a little studying. Then Juni, as his family called him, went outside again, to take the family's herd of 40 goats to forage in the nearby hills overlooking the Rio Grande.

As always Esequiel carried his .22 caliber rifle—handed down to him from his grandfather—to protect the herd from coyotes and other wild animals. What Esequiel did not know was that he himself was being stalked—not by wild animals, but by four Marines from the U.S. military's Joint Task Force Six.

The Marines were camouflaged to blend into the desert bushes, had their faces covered with black paint, and were armed with high-powered M-16 rifles. After first spotting Esequiel, the Marines followed him for 20 minutes. Then, from 200 yards away, one of the soldiers raised an M-16 to his shoulder, squeezed the trigger and shot Esequiel dead with a single bullet. It was just six days after Esequiel had turned 18.

What were these heavily armed Marines doing in the hills of Redford, practically in the backyards of the local people? What possible justification could the U.S. military have for shooting dead a Chicano high school student who was just tending to his family's livestock?

THE MILITARIZATION OF THE BORDER

The Joint Task Force Six (JTF-6) is part of the U.S. government's increasing militarization of the border with Mexico. Regular military troops are being deployed along the 2,000-mile border as part of the government's "war on immigrants" and "war on drugs."

Esequiel Hernandez Jr. was not the first person to be shot by U.S. troops on the border. Four months earlier, on January 24, Cesareo Vásquez was shot from behind by Green Berets while he was crossing the Rio Grande near Brownsville, Texas. A native of Matamoros, Mexico, Vásquez and a friend were on their way to a job in Houston tinting automobile windows.

The Border Patrol first claimed that Vásquez was a "bandit" who robbed several other immigrants, and that he was shot after firing at the soldiers with a .38 caliber revolver. But officials admitted later that Vásquez was not involved in any robbery. Vásquez said he carried a gun because he had been robbed during a previous crossing. It was a foggy night, and the camouflaged soldiers were hidden in the heavy underbrush. Vásquez explained, "I couldn't see anything. But I heard people in front of us so I fired a warning shot into the ground." The Green Berets responded by firing 11 rounds from their M-16.

There are also many immigrants who have died because the militarization of the border has forced them to cross at dangerous and remote areas in the mountains and deserts.

THE "RULES OF ENGAGEMENT"

The official explanation for the deployment of the armed forces on the border is that the troops are "assisting" the INS Border Patrol—the Migra. The soldiers are officially restricted to surveillance and reporting to the Border Patrol, and are not supposed to intervene directly.

But there is one major exception under the "rules of engagement" for these troops. They can fire—without any warning—if they are "defending" themselves.

U.S. military officials shamelessly resorted to their "rules of engagement" as justification. Defending the Marines who shot Esequiel, a Pentagon spokesman said, "Our standard rules of engagement allow the use of deadly force in self-defense."

A neighbor of the Hernandez family, who lives just down the hill from where Esequiel was killed, said, "What are these 'rules of engagement?' We had no idea we were being engaged in the first place." No one had ever told the people of Redford that the armed forces were on patrol in their area.

A DANGEROUS PRECEDENT

The deployment of the military to police the border, a job that should be performed by a beefed-up Border Patrol, would establish a dangerous precedent. If the military can be used to police border areas, why not use it to police other parts of the U.S. such as high-crime urban areas? . . .

Fortunately, we do not have to resort to police state tactics in order to quell the tide of third-world refugees to this country. Americans must inform themselves so that they will recognize the danger in such false solutions.

Robert W. Lee, *New American*, February 19, 1996.

The JTF-6 and the Marines claim that Esequiel had fired two shots from his .22 rifle and then aimed for a third shot. Only then, the story goes, did one of the troops fire his M-16. According to the perverse logic of the U.S. military, the four

Marines—armed with automatic weapons, expertly camouflaged and hidden from view—were in fear for their lives from a goat herder carrying an ancient .22 rifle.

Many things about this story are suspicious. The Marine unit followed Esequiel for 20 minutes—plenty of time to observe that he was doing nothing but looking after a few dozen goats. After they shot Esequiel, the Marines waited 22 minutes to radio for medical assistance, even though one of them was a trained medic. When a deputy sheriff first arrived on the scene, he was told that Esequiel had injured himself by falling into a well. The autopsy result was inconsistent with the version of events told by the Marines. The bullet's point of entry and path inside the body showed that Esequiel was facing *away* from the Marines when he was shot. And the people living nearby heard only one shot fired—the one that killed Esequiel.

MURDERED IN COLD BLOOD

What exactly happened is not yet clear. But the various pieces of evidence point to a strong possibility that Esequiel was murdered in cold blood.

Local officials have said that they might bring charges against the Marines who shot Esequiel. But the four soldiers were quickly whisked away to Camp Pendleton in California. A spokeswoman at the base told the *New York Times* that the four Marines had "returned to business as usual." [A Texas grand jury refused to indict the Marine for shooting Hernandez.]

At the same time, top U.S. government officials are hypocritically portraying themselves as being sympathetic to the victim and his family. After a recent talk with Esequiel's sister and others from Redford, Clinton's "drug czar" General Barry McCaffrey called the shooting a tragedy and promised an investigation.

But these high-level officials cannot wash their hands of responsibility for the killing of Esequiel. What happened in the hills of Redford is the result of the cruel anti-immigrant policies and the program of militarization of the southern border regions, directed from the top levels of the government.

Clinton brags that under his administration there has been a huge mobilization along the U.S.-Mexico border and that record numbers of immigrants have been arrested. The federal plan for the southern border region, scheduled to be unveiled in a few months, reportedly calls for a huge increase in the Border Patrol—from about 6,000 agents today to 20,000 over the next 10 years. Billions of dollars have been spent on weapons, barricades, electronic tracking equipment, ID systems, communications and police transport—creating a warlike situation all along the border. Many anti-immigrant laws are being passed on the federal and state levels. Federal welfare cuts have especially targeted immigrants.

HUNTERS CHASING PREY

It's in this climate of hate and persecution that the four Marines were secretly helicoptered into the hills of Redford—with their M-16s, night-vision goggles and other high-tech equipment. As they went about their mission, they spotted a young Latino— with a gun. For these Marines—with their training and their indoctrination—any brown-skinned person in this remote land, near a shallow crossing of the Rio Grande, was a potential enemy—an "illegal" or a "drug runner." They followed him, through the mesquite and creosote bushes, like a hunter chasing prey. And then they shot him dead.

The killing of Esequiel Hernandez Jr. was not just an "accident" or a "mistake" by four individual soldiers. It was the result of the criminal policies formulated at the highest levels of this country's ruling class.

Shortly after the shooting in Redford, La Resistencia issued a statement of condemnation which said in part: "The blood of Esequiel Hernandez is on the hands of the U.S. government. His death must compel people everywhere to resist and defeat the militarization of the border and the whole U.S. War on Immigrants."

WANTING JUSTICE

Esequiel Hernandez Sr. was gathering firewood along the banks of the Rio Grande when he heard the loud gunshot. He knew it wasn't from his son's .22. And it came from the direction of the hill where his son was tending the family's goats. He raced up the hill, past the neighbors' trailer homes. He came upon the sheriff's deputies, who asked him to identify the lifeless body on the ground.

"I don't understand it," Esequiel Hernandez Sr. said about the shooting and the military's cold-hearted response. "I want there to be justice."

Periodical Bibliography

The following articles have been selected to supplement the diverse views presented in this chapter. Addresses are provided for periodicals not indexed in the *Readers' Guide to Periodical Literature*, the *Alternative Press Index*, the *Social Sciences Index*, or the *Index to Legal Periodicals and Books*.

Jerrold B. Burnell   "Wanted: A Fair Immigration Policy,"
                        Conservative Review, May/June 1996. Available
                        from 1307 Dolley Madison Blvd., Rm. 203,
                        MacLean, VA 22101.

Mike Davis   "California Über Alles?" *Covert Action Quarterly*,
                        Spring 1995. Available from 1500
                        Massachusetts Ave. NW, #732, Washington,
                        DC 20005.

Thomas J. Espenshade   "Does the Threat of Border Apprehension
                        Deter Undocumented U.S. Immigration?"
                        Population and Development Review, December 1994.

Samuel Francis   "Immigration Control Harmed by Its Natural
                        Allies," *Conservative Chronicle*, May 1, 1996.
                        Available from Box 37077, Boone, IA 50037-
                        0077.

Glenn Garvin   "Bringing the Border War Home," *Reason*,
                        October 1995.

S.C. Gwynne   "Border Skirmish," *Time*, August 25, 1997.

John F. McManus   "Who Pays for Illegal Immigration?" *New
                        American*, January 23, 1995. Available from PO
                        Box 8040, Appleton, WI 54913.

José Palafox   "Militarizing the Border," *Covert Action Quarterly*,
                        Spring 1996.

Sharon Rhodes-Wickett   "Mistreating the Alien in Our Midst," *Christian
                        Social Action*, February 1995. Available from 100
                        Maryland Ave. NE, Washington, DC 20002.

Herman Schwartz   "Entitlements for Undocumented Aliens: Is
                        California's Proposition 187 Constitutional?
                        No: The Law Is Clear, Only the Court Has
                        Changed," *ABA Journal*, February 1995.

Dan Stein   "Yes: The Supreme Court Must Re-Evaluate
                        Existing Law," *ABA Journal*, February 1995.

Daniel W. Sutherland   "Identity Crisis," *Reason*, December 1997.

Tom Teepen   "Cracking Down on Illegal Learners," *Liberal Opinion Week*, April 22, 1996. Available from PO Box 469, Vinton, IA 52349.

Alton S. Windsor   "Restoring Our Borders: One American's Efforts," *New American*, February 19, 1997.

CHAPTER 4

HOW SHOULD U.S. IMMIGRATION POLICY BE REFORMED?

CHAPTER PREFACE

California health officials estimate that nearly 100,000 children are born each year in the state's hospitals to foreigners who are in the country illegally. According to the U.S. Constitution's Fourteenth Amendment, these babies automatically become citizens of the United States even though their parents are not. Immigration policy allows illegal aliens whose children are U.S. citizens to stay in the country; these families are also eligible for welfare entitlements such as Aid to Families with Dependent Children. Many Americans are resentful of such policies, and birthright citizenship has sparked intense debate in the halls of Congress and across the country.

Many Americans believe that such citizenship is a huge incentive for illegal immigrants to give birth in the United States, thus undercutting U.S. immigration policy. Furthermore, critics assert, the framers of the Fourteenth Amendment never intended to grant citizenship to illegal aliens, a concept that was unheard-of in 1868 when the amendment was passed. Jacob Howard, the senator who authored the amendment, originally believed it should deny birthright citizenship to "persons born in the United States who are foreigners, aliens, who belong to the families of ambassadors or foreign ministers." Reforming immigration law to include such a distinction would be better than allowing illegals to stay in the country, reformers assert.

Supporters of birthright citizenship contend, however, that few illegal immigrants come to the United States for the sole purpose of having their children born on U.S. soil. Instead, the supporters assert, immigrants come for the economic opportunities that are not available in their homeland. Therefore, they maintain, denying birthright citizenship to the children of illegal aliens will not eliminate illegal immigration. The only purpose this action would serve, they argue, is to punish the children for the misdeeds of their parents.

The large number of legal and illegal immigrants who enter and stay in the United States ensures that dissension over immigration policies will continue. The authors in the following chapter debate whether and how immigration policies affecting legal and illegal immigrants should be reformed.

| "We need to declare an immediate moratorium on immigration into the U.S.—to enable us to get the situation under control."

A MORATORIUM ON IMMIGRATION IS NEEDED

Wayne C. Lutton and John H. Tanton

In the following viewpoint, Wayne C. Lutton and John H. Tanton argue that the United States should issue an immediate moratorium on immigration until new policies can be developed. If the United States is to stabilize its population, Lutton and Tanton maintain, no more immigrants can be accepted. Lutton is a policy analyst and author of *The Immigration Time Bomb* and *The Myth of Open Borders*. Tanton is the former chairman of the National Sierra Club Population Committee, former president of Zero Population Growth, and the founder of the Federation for American Immigration Reform. He is also the author of *Rethinking Immigration Policy and Alternatives to Growth: A Search for Sustainable Futures* and the editor and publisher of the *Social Contract*, a conservative quarterly magazine.

As you read, consider the following questions:
1. To whom should immigration be limited during a moratorium, in the authors' opinion?
2. What is the purpose of immigration, according to Lutton and Tanton?
3. What three measures do the authors advocate to reduce legal and illegal immigration?

Excerpted from *The Immigration Invasion*, by Wayne C. Lutton and John H. Tanton (Petoskey, MI: Social Contract Press, 1994). Reprinted by permission of the publisher.

Developing the political consensus needed for meaningful reforms will require time. Unfortunately, we do not have much time left. That is why the authors, with their combined 50 years of study of U.S. immigration problems, have concluded that first we need to declare an immediate moratorium on immigration into the U.S.—to enable us to get the situation under control.

Only with a pause in immigration—a timeout—will we be able to coolly debate this issue, formulate strategies and implement new policies.

Throughout our history, periods of high immigration have always been followed by long breaks in the flow that provided time to assimilate recent arrivals. Such pauses in immigration occurred during the Colonial period, again through the 1860s and 1870s, and most recently from 1925 to 1965.

Since the mid–1960s, we have experienced nearly thirty years of massive, constantly expanding and uninterrupted immigration—greater than the heavy immigration between 1890 and 1914. In the last decade alone, the U.S. admitted nearly ten million legal immigrants. We believe that all the facts provide ample evidence of the need for a hiatus, a breather, a "seventh-immigration stretch" to assimilate the newcomers, to try to resolve the problems that have been created, and to consider what immigration policy we want for the future.

The first two of the earlier breaks mentioned above were not brought about as acts of deliberate public policy. They were accidents of history. However, the third one, beginning in 1917, was passed by Congress in response to popular demand.

A THIRD MORATORIUM IS NEEDED

By 1924 Congress had passed laws reducing immigration from over 1 million a year down to about 150,000. This is what needs to happen again. And it is for this type of moratorium that we specifically call—with a reduction on the same order of magnitude.

If we limited immigration to only spouses and dependent, minor, never-married children of U.S. citizens, and a few bona fide political refugees, we would skill be admitting about 200,000 persons per year . . . not as steep a cut as 1924.

As for refugees, the United States has done more than its fair share over the past fifty years, taking in more refugees for permanent resettlement than the rest of the world combined. (Many other countries take in people temporarily, until they can move on to some other country—too often the U.S.!) During the moratorium, we should call on the other signers of the UN [United

Nations] Resolution on the Status of Refugees to do their part. Strictly acting as a *temporary* haven, the United States might continue to accept a very small number of refugees.

A moratorium would give us a chance to gain control of immigration and to have the open and honest public policy debate needed to frame the type of immigration policy we want for the 21st century.

THE PURPOSES OF IMMIGRATION

First and foremost, Congress must decide on the purposes of immigration, to guide its legislative efforts. Father Hesburgh and the Select Commission on Immigration & Refugee Policy called for this in the early 1980s. Amazingly, we still do not now have such a document or consensus on exactly what we are trying to achieve. It is little wonder then that we have an inconsistent and incoherent policy, since we do not know what our objectives are.

In our view, such a statement would, as a minimum, make it clear that immigration is to serve, first and foremost, the interests of the American people. It should be subservient to other American goals for the general economy, employment, education, health, welfare, population and the environment. It would hold that illegal immigration is unacceptable and must be reduced to the practicable minimum. Finally, it would assert that We, the People (not previous immigrants nor others overseas), should determine who enters, in what numbers, and what measures will be used to enforce these limits.

Here are our ideas for a new immigration policy: . . .

The basic and most fundamental requirement for legal immigration is an overall, inclusive ceiling covering *all* classifications of entrants, including refugees and asylees.

How might we set the ceiling for the numbers to be admitted? It certainly cannot be on the basis of demand, for there are literally tens of millions, if not billions, of people who would come to the United States if they could.

HOW MANY AND WHO?

Rather, a ceiling must be set in view of our own national interests. The chief consideration, in our opinion, should be the demographic future we desire for the United States. How big do we want our population to get? And how fast do we want to get there? Of what groups do we want our population composed, and in what proportion? We need, as a nation, to debate and settle these points during the moratorium we have proposed.

During the 1970s and 1980s, picking an immigration ceiling was an easier proposition, since fertility in the U.S. was below replacement. We could afford some additions to our numbers through immigration and still look forward to stabilizing our population.

TIME FOR A MORATORIUM

Is it wise for the U.S. to continue to absorb [so many] immigrants a year? Immigration is not the sole cause of America's problems, but continued mass immigration, legal and illegal, makes existing educational, budgetary, social and economic problems much more difficult to solve. . . .

Our national leaders should practice democracy and exercise some common sense by immediately enacting a five-year moratorium on legal immigration with an all-inclusive ceiling of 100,000 a year. Such a moratorium would allow us to address existing problems and to develop a long-term, sustainable immigration policy.

Jack C. Terrazas and Yeh Ling-Ling, *Social Contract*, Summer 1996.

But now, in the 1990s, the U.S. fertility rate has gone back up to replacement level, an average of 2.1 children per couple. When population growth from immigration is added to this, it means that, if continued, the U.S. population will *never stop growing*.

We believe, as poll results suggest, that very few Americans want this. After all, our population has multiplied sixty-four times since 4 million people were counted in the first census in 1790; if it doubled two more times, we would be bigger than present-day India, nearly as large as China, with a standard of living headed in their direction.

If overall U.S. fertility rates rise above replacement, then immigration must virtually cease if we are to stabilize our population. Were this achieved, our population would continue to grow unless birthrates fell to replacement levels. Paradoxically, the main reason the U.S. birthrate has gone up is the high birthrates of recent immigrants.

THREE-HUNDRED MILLION IS ENOUGH!

Given current fertility rates, immigration must be sharply reduced if we Americans want to stabilize our numbers at 300 million—20 percent above the 1990 level of 250 million. Three hundred million Americans would be more than enough to provide any economies of scale, and might—with good planning, and a good measure of luck!—still allow us and our children to enjoy a decent quality of life for many years to come.

The alternative of perpetual population growth, with all that it implies for our political system, the environment, and the quality of our lives, is simply not acceptable.

SOME OTHER SPECIFIC MEASURES

There are many other details on legal immigration that need attention. After clearly stating the purposes of immigration policy, and setting an overall ceiling, we need to:

- Stop chain migration, where the admission of married sons and daughters or married brothers and sisters opens up the spouses' extended families to immigration. We should admit only nuclear family units: spouses of U.S. citizens and their dependent, minor, never-married children.
- End the absurdity of granting U.S. citizenship simply by virtue of being born on U.S. soil, even if the parents are illegal aliens. Scholarly opinion holds that this *does not* require a constitutional amendment.
- Deter marriage fraud, whereby an alien obtains legal resident status through a sham marriage to a U.S. citizen.
- Require foreign students to return home after their training in the U.S.
- Implement the Systematic Alien Verification for Entitlement (SAVE) program nationwide, to reduce fraudulent immigrant claims on welfare.
- Tie our immigration program to the needs of our labor market to assure that newcomers do not displace our own people in the work force. Move the administration of immigration back to the Labor Department, where it was before Franklin Roosevelt transferred it to the Justice Department in the 1940s.
- Assure that aliens do not get the right to vote until they are naturalized, and that illegal aliens are not counted for representation in our legislative bodies.
- Prohibit affirmative action benefits for immigrants.
- Give credits for knowing English in the selection of immigrants, and require English language skills in the naturalization exams that are high enough so that newly naturalized citizens can vote in English. Then repeal the bilingual ballot section of the Voting Rights Act, and end other mandated bilingual programs in education and public services.
- Fully automate the INS [Immigration and Naturalization

Service], and simplify the immigration laws so they are no longer a lucrative field for lawyers; charge adequate fees to cover the services rendered; provide citizens legal standing to sue to enforce immigration laws, and provide for a "sunset" on the basic immigration law, so that Congress must reconsider and revise it every few years (as is done with other programs) to help it conform to prevailing economic, social, and political conditions.

- Transform the Social Security card into a fraud-resistant identification document for *all* entitlement programs. Do the same for state driver's licenses (as has already been done in California).
- Close the local government-sponsored centers that help place illegal aliens in jobs.
- Finally, grant no more amnesties!

This is only a partial listing of measures that need to be taken. But enactment of these proposals would go far to achieve our goal of controlling immigration. All we need is the will to act. . . .

THE END OF THE AGE OF MIGRATION

From the dawn of human history, picking up and moving on has been a workable solution to many human problems. However, there are no longer any vacant, habitable regions to which one can run. Every liveable area is now occupied, if not to its absolute carrying capacity, at least to a level where few of the current residents will welcome any newcomers.

Of all the members of the United Nations, only a handful still take in any substantial numbers of legal immigrants, and it seems very likely that even these countries will in the near future conclude that they have reached their limit. What then?

Mass migration is no longer a solution to human problems. People will now have to stay in the land of their birth, and work to change the conditions they do not like. This is the effort that should be occupying our attention and efforts, not shuffling the deck chairs on our global Titanic.

International migration is yesterday's solution for yesterday's less-crowded world.

"Free immigration is to the long-run material self-interest of the citizens of a capitalist country."

IMMIGRATION RESTRICTIONS ARE HARMFUL

George Reisman

The argument that population growth leads to a decline in a nation's standard of living does not apply in a capitalist society, contends George Reisman in the following viewpoint. He asserts that free immigration increases the number of people working, which in turn produces a larger supply of consumer and capital goods. Reisman is a professor of economics at Pepperdine University in Malibu, California, and author of *The Government Against the Economy*.

As you read, consider the following questions:

1. When would an increase in population harm society, according to Reisman?
2. In the author's view, what is wrong with the theory that an increase in immigration results in a lower amount of capital goods per worker?
3. How do immigrants improve a country's culture, in Reisman's opinion?

Excerpted from *Capitalism: A Treatise on Economics*, by George Reisman (Ottawa, IL: Jameson Books, 1996), pp. 358–67. Copyright ©1996 by George Reisman. All rights reserved. Reprinted by permission of the author.

With the notable exceptions of Adam Smith and Frederic Bastiat, the Classical economists taught, in sympathy with Malthus, that population growth represents a threat to the average standard of living. Their belief was that the larger the number of people, the larger the amount and poorer the quality of land and mineral deposits that must be worked to support them, and, at the same time, the more intensive the exploitation of each piece of land and mineral deposit worked, resulting in diminishing returns. For both reasons, they held, increases in population and in the number of workers tend to be accompanied by less than proportionate increases in the supply of food and minerals.

The clear implication of this doctrine is that there is an inherent conflict of interests among people as their numbers increase. It is tantamount to the claim that man is in the position of the lions in the jungle after all. The lions are at the point of a scarcity of food supply; man allegedly approaches it with every increase in his numbers. Indeed, Malthus was the inspiration for Darwin, whose writings were in turn the inspiration for the doctrine of conflict of interests presented under the name Social Darwinism. A garbled form of Malthusianism is a root of the ecology movement's hostility to population growth.

The fact is, however, that the Classical economists' ideas on the effects of population growth are valid *only for a stagnant, non-division-of-labor society*. In such a society, everyone lives in the same way—namely, as a self-sufficient farmer. In such a society, the existence of more people does mean the need for more and more land of progressively inferior quality and an ever worsening problem of diminishing returns. In such a society, it does mean the need to start farms higher and higher up the sides of hills or mountains, to extend farming to rockier patches of soil, or down into marshlands, and to subdivide existing farms among more and more people—all with the result of declining yields per unit of labor expended.

A DIVISION-OF-LABOR SOCIETY

But this is not at all what the existence of more people means in a division-of-labor society. *In a division-of-labor society, a larger population means a greater, more intensive division of labor.*

Adam Smith alluded to this fact when he wrote that "the division of labor is limited by the extent of the market." The meaning of this proposition is that the extent to which the division of labor can be carried in the production of anything depends on the volume in which it is to be produced. If, for example, automobiles are to be turned out at a rate of, say, ten or twenty a day in a given location, then it is impossible that a step which takes five minutes to perform on any one car could be anyone's full-time job. The daily volume of automobile production would have to be increased to approximately one hundred in a given location before such an operation could be made into a full-time job. (One hundred times five minutes equals eight and one-third hours, which represents a full-time job.) The daily volume of automobile production would have to be increased to approximately one thousand in a given location, before an operation requiring only thirty seconds could be made into a full-time job, and so on. (One thousand times thirty seconds also equals eight and one-third hours.) Thus, the larger the volume to be produced—the larger the market to be served—the further can the division of labor be carried. . . .

FREE IMMIGRATION

It is necessary to address the issue of free immigration, which is closely related to the subject of population growth. Free immigration is to the long-run material self-interest of the citizens of a capitalist country.

The words *capitalist country* must be stressed. To the extent that a country has a welfare system, tax-supported hospitals and schools, public housing, and so on, and the immigrants come to take advantage of these offerings, the effect is a corresponding loss to the present inhabitants of the country, who have to pay the costs. The above proposition applies to a country insofar as it is *without* these and other welfare-state-type programs—a country in which the immigrants must be self-supporting and themselves pay for whatever they receive. By the same token, the freedom of a country implies the absence of economic disabilities imposed on immigrants: there are no minimum-wage laws or prounion legislation to prevent them from gaining employment, and no legal obstacles to their starting businesses, buying land, and so on.

Under such conditions, the freedom of immigration must ultimately prove economically beneficial to everyone. Among the immigrants and their descendants will be individuals of great talent, capable of achieving great things in a free country, but who would be stifled and be able to contribute little or nothing in the lands of their origin. In effect, the freedom of immigration into a free country from countries that are less free or unfree is a vital means of *unlocking human talent and increasing the gains from the pyramid of ability.*

As a simple example, one should consider what would have been the effect on Andrew Carnegie, and not just on the American but on the world steel industry, if he had been prevented from immigrating to the United States and confined to the less free environment of Scotland and Great Britain. One should consider what would have been the effect on the development of the helicopter if Sikorsky had been prevented from immigrating to the United States from Russia. Is it likely that the Russians would have seen the value of his ideas before they had been proved by actual repeated demonstration in the United States?

Indeed, we should consider the effects if the *ancestors* of any American industrial innovator had had to remain in their native lands, and thus that person had been born and spent his life in a country like Italy, Poland, Russia, or Germany, or even France or Great Britain, instead of the United States. Probably most of the innovators would have been stifled or at least significantly held back.

ECONOMIC FREEDOM

The historical fact that the people of the United States had access to more business talent than the people of any European country was due to America's policy of greater economic freedom in general combined with her policy of free immigration in particular. The latter gave the United States a larger population from which to draw such talent, while the former ensured that in the larger population *a greater frequency of such talent would be manifested*, because freedom is the essential condition for the development and flowering of such talent. The combination of free immigration and general economic freedom thus results both in more people *and*, at the same time, as an inextricable part of the same process, *a rate of economic progress that is not only rapid, but also further accelerated by virtue of the immigration.* Simply put, free immigration into a free country accelerates economic progress, *because talent requires freedom in order to flourish. Free immigration into a free country brings talent to freedom, and so enables more of it to develop and contribute to economic progress.* The acceleration of economic progress it achieves ultimately far outstrips whatever short-run problems may accompany an increase in immigration. . . .

[The main economic argument against free immigration is] that a larger population must reduce the productivity of labor because it means a higher ratio of labor to capital goods, or, what is the same thing, less capital goods per worker. Those who advance this argument believe that population growth and increases in the supply of capital goods are independent processes. Capital accumulation, they believe, is determined simply by saving, which allegedly has no connection with the growth of population.

No Reasonable Case

The fact is that a larger number of people working and producing *is itself the cause of a larger supply of capital goods*. A larger number of people working and producing in conjunction even with an unchanged supply of capital goods results in an increase in total production. This no one can deny. It is only necessary to realize that what is produced in an economy is not only consumers' goods, but also *capital goods*. Labor and existing capital goods are used to produce both consumers' goods *and* capital goods, and they do so in accordance with the relative demands for the two types of goods.

The implication of this is that if there is any single, one-time increase in the number of people working and producing, it automatically tends to be followed by a growth in the supply of capital goods per worker and thus in output per worker at least back to their original levels. For the larger number of workers produces more capital goods with which that same larger number of workers then works in the next period, and with the aid of which it enjoys a higher productivity. The further effect is another increase in production in the following period—both of consumers' goods *and* of capital goods, until the original levels of capital goods per worker and the productivity of labor are equalled and, indeed, surpassed.

Thus, it should be clear that no reasonable case exists against any single dose of immigration or population increase based on the argument that it reduces the amount of capital goods per worker. For the additional labor itself results in progressively more capital goods.

Another Argument Has No Standing

In the case of a continuous increase in the supply of labor, it could be argued that just as the first group of additional workers brings about an increase in the supply of capital goods, a second group arrives on the scene, so that the ratio of capital goods to labor does not increase and may even fall further. Yet even this more sophisticated version of the reduced-capital-per-worker argument against immigration and population growth cannot stand. If the productivity of labor were threatened by a relative excess of labor and a relative deficiency of capital goods, the effect would be a drop in the demand for labor, and thus in the wage earners' demand for consumers' goods, and a rise in the demand for capital goods. The effect of this, in turn, would be a higher relative production of capital goods and a lower relative production of consumers' goods. The larger number of workers of each year would find sufficient additional capital goods available because they would be produced by *a larger proportion of the labor and capital goods of each year*, as well as by a growing volume of labor and capital goods from year to year.

And, as time went on, the positive effects of the unlocking of more human talent would occur. The effect of this would be an increase in the output of capital goods (and consumers' goods) that can be obtained from any given quantity of labor working in conjunction with any given quantity of capital goods. Even if it occurred on a strictly delimited, once-and-for-all basis, the effect of this in turn would be a more rapid rate of increase in the production both of capital goods and consumers' goods, with each year's larger output of capital goods serving as the base for the following year's further increase in the production both of capital goods and of consumers' goods.

Thus, a capitalist economy with the freedom of immigration turns out in the long run to have a more rapid rate of capital accumulation than one without it. For it has both a larger relative production of capital goods and uses capital goods more efficiently in the further production of capital goods than one without the freedom of immigration. The effect of this more rapid rate of capital accumulation is a correspondingly faster rate of economic progress, which soon makes up for the reduction in the proportion of output going to the consumption of wage earners. . . .

ASSIMILATION

[Another] objection to the freedom of immigration is a non-economic argument to the effect that it means turning the country over to foreigners and thus destroying its language and culture. The fact is that for a capitalist country the *opposite* is true. The freedom of immigration is the principal means of extending the language and culture of such a country. For the immigrants come voluntarily, in order to take advantage of freedom and to benefit themselves. They come with the knowledge that they are coming to a better country than the one they left behind, and so are well-disposed to learning its language and absorbing its culture. And because they come from many different lands, each with its own language, the language of the new country is the logical common ground for them to choose in dealing with one another. Learning it is also virtually indispensable for practical success, since almost all of the existing wealth of the country is in the hands either of its native inhabitants or of earlier immigrants who have learned the language to be able to deal with the native inhabitants. It was in just this way that English came to be the language of tens of millions of people who originally did not speak English—people who, along with learning English, made the most important parts of Anglo-Saxon culture their own, such as the idea of the rule of law and the sanctity of private property.

THE CASE FOR FREE IMMIGRATION

One of the best cases in favor of immigration is the Cuban miracle in Miami, Florida. . . . In the early 1960s some 200,000 penurious immigrants thronged this stagnant urban community, more than the total black unemployed youths in all America's urban areas at the time. It was the most rapid and overwhelming migration to one American city. Few spoke English and virtually none had jobs or housing. Yet in less than a decade, these Cuban immigrants revived Miami's stagnant inner city and transformed the entire Miami economy.

Mark Skousen, *Freeman*, September 1995.

The immigrants, of course, do not merely absorb their new country's culture. They help to make it better. They contribute to it not only all their business, scientific, and artistic achievements, and what is valuable in their own heritage, but, perhaps most important of all, a constantly renewed sense of personal ambition and personal achievement. They are a fresh inspiration in every generation.

The fact that while two hundred years ago English was the native language of perhaps twelve million people out of a world population of one billion, and is today the native language of over three hundred and fifty million people out of a world population of about four billion, is due principally to the existence of the freedom of immigration into the United States. The ability of the United States to become the leading economic and military power in the world would not have been possible without its freedom of immigration, which both attracted the numbers and powerfully contributed to their per capita productivity. Had the United States adhered to its policy of free immigration— along with the rest of its freedom—it is probable that today it would have a population approximately twice as large and a standard of living at least twice as high as the population and

standard of living it presently has. As such, it would so far sur-
pass any combination of external powers as to be absolutely
unassailable.

ECONOMIC PROGRESS

The discussion of free immigration that has just been presented
implies the necessity of modifying an important proposition of
economics—namely, the proposition that the movement of
workers from lower-paying to higher-paying jobs brings about
an equalization of wage rates. This proposition must be limited
to a context in which the jobs are performed *under the same degree of
economic freedom and cultural rationality.* The movement of workers
from lower-paying jobs in less-free, less-rational countries to
higher-paying jobs in a freer, more-rational country does not
equalize wage rates, but increases the differences still further, because the productivity of labor in the freer, more rational country will tend to grow all the more rapidly relative to the productivity of labor in the other countries, thanks to the unlocking of
human talent and the capital formation that is brought about in
the freer, more-rational country. Thus, free immigration con-
tributes to the emergence of virtually two different worlds, as
population moves from politically created wastelands into countries in which freedom and rationality make possible continuous
economic progress.

It should now be clear that the freedom of immigration into
a capitalist country is to the long-run economic self-interest of
all of its inhabitants. It enables more talent to flourish and thus
increases the rate of economic progress in that country, through
the greater operation of the pyramid-of-ability principle.

> "The United States ought to revise the criteria for admission to ... [allow] immigrants to come pretty much on a first-come, first-served basis."

REFORM IMMIGRATION POLICY BY CHANGING THE PREFERENCE SYSTEM

Peter D. Salins

Peter D. Salins argues in the following viewpoint that the current immigration quota system encourages family reunification while skewing the nationality mix of immigrants. Salins proposes a new immigration policy that would grant visas on a first-come, first-serve basis. Such a system would assure that the granting of immigration visas would be fairer and more random than the current system, he contends. Furthermore, he argues, a first-come, first-serve basis would assure that the most motivated immigrants would immigrate to the United States. Salins is the author of *Assimilation, American Style*, from which this viewpoint is excerpted.

As you read, consider the following questions:

1. What are the three key categories for admitting immigrants to the United States, according to Salins?
2. In the author's opinion, how would a skills-based immigration policy harm the American economy?
3. Why is America's refugee and asylee system unfair, in Salins's view?

Excerpts and notes from *Assimilation, American Style*, by Peter D. Salins. Copyright ©1997 by BasicBooks. Reprinted by permission of BasicBooks, a division of HarperCollins Publishers, Inc.

As it stands, American immigration policy, underneath its ever-changing surface complexity, is heavily skewed in its criteria for deciding whom, among the millions applying each year, to admit. Consistently and clearly favored are applicants in three key categories: those who are relatives of American citizens and residents, those who are fleeing political or religious persecution, and those who are in valued professions and occupations. Applicants in these generic categories are given "preference" according to several hierarchical principles. Relatives of citizens are preferred to relatives of permanent residents. Among relatives, spouses, minor children, and parents are preferred over married children and siblings. Among occupations, highly educated professionals like physicians and engineers are preferred to those in less skilled occupations. Refugees from certain designated countries (such as those fleeing Communist dictatorships) have been preferred to people who randomly request asylum. These preferences are embedded in an aggregate annual immigration quota of about 700,000, exclusive of refugees and those seeking asylum. In addition, the number of immigrants after 1988 was swollen by the amnesty of illegal immigrants who were given legal immigrant status under the Immigration Reform and Control Act of 1986 (IRCA). All told, the United States has admitted between 600,000 and 900,000 immigrants a year since 1986, not counting the illegal immigrants who received amnesty under the IRCA.

FAMILY REUNIFICATION

By far the largest number of immigrants admitted each year fall under the general category of "family reunification," which reflects an overwhelming policy bias toward relatives of American residents over all other applicants. In 1993, nearly 500,000 of the 700,000 regular immigration places were reserved for family members. When the "national origins" basis of prevailing immigration policy was overturned in 1965, the explicit justification for grounding the new system in family-based immigration preferences was that it would favor European immigrants. Since most Americans had European roots, it was supposed that most immigrants who would be admitted under a family-preference system would naturally be Europeans. Americans were prepared for the arrival of more Italians and Greeks and fewer English and Germans than under the old quota system, but they expected the net effect to be pro-European.

Events did not turn out that way because by the 1960s most Europeans—even Italians and Greeks—lived in countries that were enjoying newfound political stability and prosperity. So although Europeans immigrated to the United States in somewhat greater numbers after 1965 than they did before, they hardly exhausted the more generous immigration quotas of the new policy. If Europeans no longer found going to America so compelling after 1965, Latin Americans, Asians, and people from the Caribbean did. In the two decades before the new immigration policy, 55 percent of all immigrants came from Europe, 22 percent from Latin America and the Caribbean, and 5 percent from Asia. In the two decades afterward, 13 percent of all immigrants were European, 45 percent were Latin or Caribbean, and 37 percent were Asian.

Initially, the new system attracted immigrants from a broad cross section of nationalities, but over time the idiosyncrasies of the preference system have skewed the nationality mix toward immigrants from just a handful of countries. In 1993, fifteen countries accounted for nearly 70 percent of all immigrants, and Mexico alone contributed 14 percent. The other countries in the top ten are China, the Philippines, Vietnam, the former Soviet Union, the Dominican Republic, India, Poland, El Salvador, and the United Kingdom. The various nationalities owe their immigration quotas, however, to different features of current immigration policy. Applicants from Vietnam and the former Soviet Union are the most important beneficiaries of refugee preferences. Most immigrants from other countries come under one or another family preference. . . .

AN IMPERFECT SYSTEM

America's legal immigration system is . . . far from ideal. Indeed, there is probably no desirable paradigm or formula for "designing" the mix of immigrants. Every attempt to find one since the United States first developed a comprehensive immigration policy in the 1920s has been unsatisfactory. The national-origins concept, which was introduced in the Immigration Act of 1924 and sustained though the McCarran-Walter Act of 1952, was explicitly—and shamefully—discriminatory toward particular nationalities and racist to the core. The family-preference system, which has been the foundation of American immigration policy since 1965, while superficially attractive (who wants to argue against reuniting families?) has been degenerating into a latter-day version of the national-origins system by increasingly skewing immigration toward the nationalities of recent immigrants. Although this system is not generating the nationality mix that was originally envisioned, it is having precisely the effect that the architects of the 1965 immigration reforms anticipated: biasing the immigrant mix toward those nationalities that are already heavily represented.

IMMIGRATION, BY COUNTRY OF ORIGIN					
Country	1820–60	1861–90	1891–1930	1931–70	1971–91
Ireland	1,956,000	1,528,000	1,084,000	112,000	48,000
Germany	1,546,000	2,958,000	1,402,000	1,010,000	177,000
Norway/Sweden	36,000	888,000	1,088,000	108,000	27,000
United Kingdom	794,000	1,962,000	1,479,000	588,000	313,000
Italy	13,000	375,000	4,263,000	525,000	226,000
Poland	2,000	67,000	330,000	89,000	137,000
Russia/Soviet Union	1,000	255,000	3,085,000	5,000	129,000
Other European	2,261,000	1,039,000	5,665,000	981,000	652,000
China	41,000	249,000	87,000	67,000	495,000
Other Asian	1,000	10,000	671,000	568,000	4,173,000
Canada	117,000	931,000	1,849,000	1,072,000	347,000
Mexico	18,000	9,000	729,000	837,000	3,244,000
Other American	47,000	57,000	484,000	1,319,000	3,305,000

Peter D. Salins, *Assimilation, American Style*, 1997.

Many proponents of immigration reforms advocate instead a "designer" immigration policy that would favor skilled and professional workers, a bias that dominates Canada's immigration policy (which also favors applicants with substantial financial resources), and is found in the lower tiers of the current American preference system. Although such a policy may guarantee a more affluent immigrant population and minimize the likelihood of immigrants being a "burden" to this country, it completely undercuts America's historic role as "the land of the new beginning," the philosophical foundation for allowing immigration in the first place. A skills-based policy would perversely vest the privilege of American immigration in those who have been the most privileged in their homelands, those with the least need to emigrate. Such a policy may not even be beneficial to the American economy because there is probably a greater need for immigrant workers at the bottom of the labor market than for immigrant professionals at the top.

REFUGEES AND ASYLEES

Another long-standing feature of American immigration policy has granted a certain number of places to refugees—persons who are seeking to flee their countries because of "a well-founded fear of being persecuted for reasons of race, religion, nationality, membership of a particular social group or political opinion"—and "asylees," refugees who have succeeded in escaping. In other words, you are a refugee if the United States grants you permission to immigrate before you leave your country and an asylee if you apply for legal immigrant status after you get here. As the policies on refugees and asylees have actually been applied by the United States, you are a refugee if you seek to leave a Communist dictatorship and an asylee if you have fled some other kind of authoritarian regime. This aspect of America's immigration-preference system is particularly subject to misapplication because it depends heavily on changing and arbitrary standards of political and personal discretion and, for most of the post–World War II period, has been merely an instrument of cold war politics. Millions of Europeans who needed a haven from German genocide in the early 1940s were turned away (and subsequently slaughtered), but those who applied from selected nations of the Communist bloc in subsequent decades—Hungarians in the 1950s, Cubans in the 1960s, Vietnamese in the 1970s, and Russians in the 1980s—were admitted with alacrity whether they were in any immediate danger or not. The political bias of the policy of giving preference to refugees and asylees continues to this day: No regime in Haiti is ever murderous enough to make more Haitians eligible as refugees, and no African country's policies of persecution or mutilation are ever cruel enough to make Africans eligible as asylees, but as long as Fidel Castro is in power, Cubans will continue to be welcome. . . .

A More Random System

Perhaps the most important change that an assimilationist immigration policy might include is to make the criteria for admitting immigrants fairer and more random. This change would allow more people without family connections to come to the United States and, in the process, would draw immigrants from a much broader array of countries. The precedent for doing so is already established because the present law has a small allotment of immigration places, awarded by lottery, specifically geared to promoting geographic diversity. The United States ought to revise the criteria for admission to enlarge this category substantially while it scales back family and refugee preferences, dispenses with skills-based allotments, and allows most immigrants to come pretty much on a first-come, first-served basis. The historic mission of American immigration would be better served by allowing more of the world's most motivated immigrants—not just those who are lucky enough to have American relatives or to have received a good education—to realize the American Dream, and the prospects for assimilation would be enhanced in the bargain.

How might such a policy work? In 1993, about 200,000 of the 500,000 immigrants admitted under family sponsorship were spouses or children of Americans, in other words, immediate relatives with the most compelling claim to family reunification. Another 130,000 immigrants who were already in the United States had their status "adjusted" as refugees and asylees in 1993. Assuming the adoption of a 1997 aggregate immigration cap of 900,000 (after 150,000 places were subtracted for illegal immigrants), one could set aside 200,000 places for immediate relatives and another 100,000 places for refugees and asylees and still leave about 600,000 places available for a dramatically enlarged allotment of immigrants based on geographic diversity. Right now the small diversity quota of 33,000 is awarded by lottery. A fairer approach might be to put all diversity applicants on a worldwide waiting list, their status reviewed and approved at American immigration centers in each country. To avoid having the worldwide diversity quota swamped by applicants from the largest countries (China and India could preempt 40 percent of all places), perhaps no nation's quota should exceed some percentage of the total. Applicants should also be screened to determine their motivation for immigrating, their health, and any criminal or other unsavory facts in their background. However the details of a first-come, first-served admissions process were developed, the objective of such a process would be to offer the privilege of immigration to the most highly motivated candidates from the most diverse pool of applicants, selected by the fairest and most objective criteria. . . .

A Generous Policy

It is to Americans' great credit that the U.S. immigration policy is as generous and enlightened as it is. What other nation in the world is willing to accept a million foreigners a year, on any terms? A few countries are periodically inundated with refugees from unstable countries next door, but those refugees aren't immigrants, and the countries they flee to don't treat them like immigrants. America's liberal immigration policy is all of a piece with its liberal political traditions in general; it was born of those traditions and, in turn, reinforces them.

But even Americans can be made to doubt from time to time

the wisdom or efficacy of their liberal immigration traditions. Happily, most Americans are aware enough of the economic and cultural contributions of immigrants that they will not easily be deflected from their tolerance of immigration by neonativists and restrictionists who are working to change the thrust of immigration policy. But nothing over the years—not even concrete economic benefits—has so solidified support for America's immigration experiment as the successful assimilation of its immigrants: assimilation, American style. As the country's citizens and politicians continue to debate immigration policy in the days ahead and to fine-tune the criteria regarding how many, and which, immigrants to admit, they must keep faith with America's two most powerful icons of immigration: the Statue of Liberty, which declares that immigrants are always welcome, and the melting pot, which says that immigrants must always assimilate.

4

| "Selling immigration slots tends to attract the most able immigrants and those who can contribute most to American society."

REFORM IMMIGRATION POLICY BY SELLING VISAS

Edward P. Lazear

In the following viewpoint, Edward P. Lazear contends that selling immigration visas is preferential to the current policy of quotas. He contends that selling visas would result in a more even distribution of immigrants from various countries. In addition, Lazear asserts, selling visas would generate income for the American treasury while reducing welfare expenditures because immigrants wealthy enough to pay their own way would be less likely to need welfare. Furthermore, he maintains, only those with a strong desire to immigrate to the United States would be willing to pay for their visas. Lazear, a senior fellow at the Hoover Institution, a research and public policy think tank in Stanford, California, is the Jack Steele Parker Professor of Human Resources Management and Economics at Stanford University's School of Business.

As you read, consider the following questions:

1. What are some of the minor problems associated with selling immigration visas, in Lazear's opinion?
2. According to the author, what is a good starting point for a price for immigration visas?
3. Why is the notion that the United States was settled by poor immigrants inaccurate, in Lazear's view?

Policies that lead to a more balanced distribution of immigrants by country of origin would reduce the amount of geographic clustering, with immigrants forming enclaves or ghettoes, and instead speed assimilation. To accomplish this, a conscious policy of country quotas, which would limit the number of immigrants from any one country in a given year, could be instituted. This would result in the desired distribution of immigrants by country of origin, but there are some disadvantages.

First of all, the quotas may be incorrect. Some countries may have large queues of individuals wanting to enter the United States, and other countries may not be able to fill their quotas. Second, individual American citizens may have preferences over not only the distribution of immigrants by country of origin but also on their identities. A quota-based system does not guarantee that relatives or friends of American citizens would be shown any preference.

SELLING IMMIGRATION SLOTS

For these reasons, a better solution is to sell immigration slots.

Selling immigration slots has a number of virtues: It would be more likely to promote balanced immigration. It generates revenue for current American citizens. It tends to favor those who have very strong desires to enter the United States over those who have only weak preferences for coming. In the same vein, it would allow current U.S. citizens who have strong preferences that certain individuals be admitted to reveal the intensity of their desire by their willingness to pay for an immigration slot.

Selling visas would result in more-balanced immigration. When immigrants have to pay significant sums for their visas, they will tend to be distributed more evenly across countries. It is unlikely that any one country would have a large enough supply of individuals who would want to immigrate to the United States at the specified price. Residents of rich countries would be better able to afford the fee, but residents of rich countries are also less inclined to come because their alternatives are better at home. There is little danger that we would end up with too many Swiss immigrants.

Selling immigration slots tends to attract the most able immigrants and those who can contribute most to American society and who are most complementary with the group of current American citizens. The individuals who are willing to pay the most to obtain entry to the United States are those who feel that they can get the most out of being here. These individuals are likely to be more educated, more able, younger, and higher producers than a random selection of immigrants. This spillover to current American citizens is also likely to be greater from this group.

A system of selling visas generates income for the current American population. As such, it is likely to reduce the hostility toward new immigrants and toward policies that do not reduce rates of immigration. Immigrants who buy their way in are also likely to be wealthier and less likely to take advantage of the current safety net, which reduces the drain on American citizens and, again, hostility toward immigrants.

MINOR PROBLEMS

The scheme is not perfect for a number of reasons. First, even if slots are sold, the market price of immigration must be determined. This will dictate the number of individuals who are willing to immigrate to the United States so that a decision of price and quantity of immigrants must be made. The government is still going to be involved in making that decision, and it is hardly clear that bureaucrats will choose prices in a way that maximizes the benefits to society. Second, there will still be a tendency for immigrants who have large support groups currently in the United States to want to come. Thus, selling immigration slots still biases immigration in favor of those countries that are well represented in the United States. This in itself is not bad, except that immigrants from large-country enclaves are less likely to become assimilated and to learn English. My sense is that this is a minor problem, given the fact that the fee is likely to be sufficiently high to attract only a relatively able group of individuals.

The system requires that an entry fee be set. As a target number, around $30,000 per immigrant might be a useful starting point. Immigrants who could pay this amount are less likely to end up going on welfare, and even if they do they have borne much of the cost up front. Second, although relatively steep, a price in this neighborhood is equivalent to the price of an expensive automobile. Most current U. S. citizens can raise or borrow the money to make a purchase of this sort, and many would be able to provide assistance for their relatives. Also, the relatives that would be most likely to be sponsored would be those who current American citizens felt would be most likely to repay the loan. This, too, would act as a beneficial screen on the immigrant population.

IMMIGRANTS WERE NOT DESTITUTE

Some may be concerned that charging immigrants would bias immigration against the poor and, in this way, disavow any belief in the famous inscription on the Statue of Liberty. There is no denying that a monetary price discourages immigration of those who cannot raise the money to enter. But the notion that the United States was made up of poor immigrants, although fashionable, is inaccurate. Passage to the United States in times past was a significant barrier to immigration. Most of our ancestors who came to the United States may have been poor by American standards but were not the poorest members of their communities. They were merchants, craftsmen, and the young and resourceful, who could raise the money to travel to and settle in the United States. It has become cheaper, not more expensive, to migrate to the United States. Indeed, it has been argued persuasively that the flow of immigrants to the United States has declined in relative income and education over the past twenty years. This is a natural result of changes in immigration policies and declining costs of transportation.

Still, choosing the right price for immigration slots is a difficult matter. Once the price is chosen, the number of immigrants is determined. Higher prices will result in fewer immigrants; lower prices will result in more immigrants. It is possible, conceptually, to think about an optimal level of immigration. Given the historical record, a flow of somewhere between a half million and a million per year might be the initial target. Over the long run, the optimal number depends in part on changes in the population through births and deaths and on the costs of assimilation. Charging for immigration is likely to raise the desired number of immigrants because money is collected when immigrants enter.

"It defies logic to insist that an illegal act on the part of parents can confer the boon of citizenship upon their children."

THE UNITED STATES SHOULD REPEAL BIRTHRIGHT CITIZENSHIP FOR CHILDREN OF ILLEGAL IMMIGRANTS

Edward J. Erler

The Fourteenth Amendment, which grants citizenship to all persons born in the United States, was added to the Bill of Rights in 1868 to overturn a Supreme Court decision that denied citizenship to all blacks of African descent. In the following viewpoint, Edward J. Erler argues that it is inappropriate to use this amendment to extend citizenship to all babies born in the United States, even when they are the children of aliens or foreigners. It is illogical, he maintains, to reward a mother's illegal immigration with the right of U.S. citizenship for her children. Congress has the right to restrict citizenship only to those who are legal residents of the United States, Erler contends. Erler is a professor of political science at California State University in San Bernardino, a senior fellow of the Claremont Institute for the Study of Statesmanship and Political Philosophy in Claremont, California, and a member of the California Advisory Commission on Civil Rights.

As you read, consider the following questions:

1. In Erler's opinion, what is the meaning of the clause "subject to the jurisdiction thereof"?
2. Why were Native Americans exempt from receiving birthright citizenship, according to Erler?
3. In the author's view, what justifies the denial of birthright citizenship for babies of illegal aliens?

Excerpted from "Immigration and Citizenship," by Edward J. Erler, in *Loyalty Misplaced: Misdirected Virtue and Social Disintegration*, edited by Gerald Frost (London Social Affairs Unit, 1997). Reprinted by permission of the author. Original endnotes have been omitted here.

It is beyond any possibility of doubt that the power to regulate immigration is an aspect of national sovereignty. Many years ago the Supreme Court remarked that "it is an accepted maxim of international law, that every sovereign nation has the power, as inherent in sovereignty, and essential to self-preservation, to forbid the entrance of foreigners within its dominions, or to admit them only in such cases and upon such conditions a[s] it may see fit to prescribe." Surely an aspect of sovereignty is not only the right to control borders, but also the right to distinguish between citizens and non-citizens. . . .

THE QUESTION OF CITIZENSHIP

Although the Constitution uses the terms "citizens of the United States" and "natural born citizen," citizenship is nowhere defined in the Constitution. This may have been because any attempt at definition would have raised the divisive question of whether or not slaves were to be considered citizens (Jefferson had referred to slaves in 1783 as "one half of our citizens"). Agitation over this issue in the Constitutional Convention would certainly have made it much more difficult to reach the compromises necessary to produce the Constitution—and without the Constitution there was little hope that slavery could ever be put, in Abraham Lincoln's words, "in the course of ultimate extinction."

Americans have always seemed somewhat ambivalent on the question of citizenship. After all, America was founded on an appeal to universal principles—"the laws of nature and of nature's God." The founding of a particular nation on universal principles—the recognition of the natural rights of all human beings—has provided something of a tension in American political life. While the nation must be committed to the single-minded protection of the rights of its own citizens, it also, in some sense, has an obligation in its own affairs to recognize the rights of mankind.

Who, then, are citizens of the regime based on universal principles? In one sense, it is all those who subscribe to those principles and have acquired the habits, manners, and industry suitable for free human beings. It is clear that a nation based on universal principles must somehow stand as an example to the world—an example that free government is possible. But even the regime based on universal principles is a particular regime; while it may have an obligation to serve as an example to the world, its primary obligation is the protection of its citizens and their way of life.

The Fourteenth Amendment (1868) was the first definition

of citizen to make its appearance in the Constitution:

> All persons born or naturalized in the United States, and subject to the jurisdiction thereof, are citizens of the United States and of the state wherein they reside.

The immediate purpose of the citizenship clause was to overturn the infamous *Dred Scott* decision of 1857 which had proclaimed all blacks of African descent to be ineligible for citizenship. Prior to the Fourteenth Amendment, federal citizenship was an incident of state citizenship; every citizen of a state was, by virtue of that citizenship, automatically a citizen of the United States. The Fourteenth Amendment reversed this relationship.

The principal object of the Fourteenth Amendment therefore was to secure federal citizenship for the newly freed slaves and extend to them the whole panoply of civil rights that are the necessary incidents of federal citizenship. In order to forestall attacks upon the citizenship of the former slaves, the framers of the Fourteenth Amendment made federal citizenship primary and state citizenship derivative, so that any person who was a citizen of the United States was automatically a citizen of the state wherein he resided. This made it impossible for the states to circumvent federal protection for civil rights by withholding state citizenship from the former slaves and thus preventing them from becoming citizens of the United States.

Even though it is clear that the Fourteenth Amendment was passed principally to settle the question of the citizenship of the newly freed slaves, today the phrase "All persons born or naturalized in the United States" is almost universally understood to confer citizenship upon all persons who are born in the United States regardless of whether they are legally in the country or not.

SUBJECT TO THE JURISDICTION THEREOF

What is the meaning of the subordinate clause in the first sentence of the Fourteenth Amendment ("subject to the jurisdiction thereof")? It is clear that, whatever else it means, it was intended to limit or qualify "All persons born or naturalized . . ." Only those persons "born or naturalized" and "subject to the jurisdiction" of the United States are citizens of the United States. Thus the phrase clearly does not have universal application. To assume, as many today do, that all persons born in the United States are automatically subject to the jurisdiction of the United States by virtue of their birth within its geographical boundaries would render the jurisdiction clause superfluous. But no constitutional interpretation can render any part of the Constitution superfluous or leave any provision without force. This is a necessary consequence of a written constitution. Any interpretation that renders a provision of the Constitution superfluous or without force would be tantamount to an amendment of the Constitution itself.

The legislative debates decisively demonstrate that both clauses of the first section of the Fourteenth Amendment were intended to have independent force. Lyman Trumbull, Chairman of the Senate Judiciary Committee and a powerful supporter of the Fourteenth Amendment, remarked on May 30, 1866, that the limiting clause refers to those "Not owing allegiance to anybody else. . . . It is only those persons who come completely within our jurisdiction, who are subject to our laws, that we think of making citizens; and there can be no objection to the proposition that such persons should be citizens." This, of course, was familiar language. The Civil Rights Act of 1866 had defined citizens of the United States as "all persons born in the United States, and not subject to any foreign power, excluding Indians not taxed." It is universally agreed that the immediate impulse for the passage of the Fourteenth Amendment was to constitutionalize the Civil Rights Act of 1866. This was an attempt to put the question of citizenship and matters of federal civil rights beyond the reach of simple congressional majorities. Thus it is clear that the idea of allegiance ("not subject to any foreign power") was somehow central to understanding the jurisdiction clause of the Fourteenth Amendment.

CITIZENSHIP AND THE CONSENT OF THE GOVERNED

Senator Jacob Howard, the author of the citizenship clause, made the most precise statement about the character of the limitation contained in the "jurisdiction" clause:

> [E]very person born within the limits of the United States, and subject to their jurisdiction, is by virtue of natural law and national law a citizen of the United States. This will not, of course, include persons born in the United States who are foreigners, aliens, who belong to the families of ambassadors or foreign ministers accredited to the Government of the United States, but will include every other class of persons. It settles the great question of citizenship and removes all doubt as to what persons are or are not citizens of the United States. This has long been a great desideratum in the jurisprudence and legislation of this country.

Clearly, the author of the citizenship clause intended to count "foreigners," "aliens," and those born to "ambassadors or foreign ministers" as outside the "jurisdiction of the United States."

But perhaps just as revealing is the fact that Howard refers both to "natural law" and "national law." As Howard surely knew, citizenship based on natural law meant that no person could be governed—or become a citizen—without his consent. This was the natural law principle of the Declaration of Independence that proclaimed that legitimate governments derive "their just powers from the consent of the governed."

SOCIAL CONTRACT REQUIRES MUTUAL CONSENT

It is certainly true that just government requires the unanimous consent of each and every individual who is to be governed, whether that consent is given explicitly or tacitly. The foundation of community based on the consent of the governed is the social contract. The common understanding of these foundations during the founding era was expressed in the Massachusetts Bill of Rights (1780):

> The end of the institution, maintenance, and administration of government, is to secure the existence of the body-politic, to protect it, and to furnish the individuals who compose it with the power of enjoying in safety and tranquillity their natural rights . . . and whenever these great objects are not obtained, the people have a right to alter the government. . . . The body-politic is formed by a voluntary association of individuals; it is a social compact by which *the whole people covenants with each citizen and each citizen with the whole people* that all shall be governed by certain laws for the common good. It is the duty of the people, therefore, in framing a constitution of government, to provide for an equitable mode of making laws, as well as for an impartial interpretation and a faithful execution of them; that every man may, at all times, find his security in them.

Thus, the social contract requires *reciprocal consent*. Not only must the individual consent to be governed, but he must also be accepted by the community as a whole. If all persons born within the geographical limits of the United States are to be counted citizens—even those whose parents are in the United States illegally—then this would be tantamount to the conferral of citizenship without the consent of "the whole people."

But if the natural law requirements of citizenship mean anything, it must surely mean that consent must be reciprocal—allegiance on the part of those who seek to become citizens and the consent of the nation. Any contract requires at least two parties; there can be no contract that binds someone who has not been party to the contract. Any reasonable person would have to agree that "subject to the jurisdiction of the United States" means those who are within the geographical limits of the country legally—that is, with the permission of the United States. Indeed, on at least one occasion the Supreme Court rightly noted that the jurisdiction requirement of the Fourteenth Amendment embodied "the principle that no one can become a citizen of a nation without its consent." The jurisdiction clause of the Fourteenth Amendment, as Howard noted, is truly the "national law" confirming or codifying the "natural law."

NORTH AMERICAN INDIANS AND THE QUESTION OF JURISDICTION

Much of the debate about the jurisdiction clause in the Congress centered on the status of Indians. The immediate question was whether the Fourteenth Amendment would confer citizenship upon the Indians as well as upon the newly freed slaves. The former slaves, of course, had been born in the United States and had always been subject to its jurisdiction. Was the same true of Indians? Indians were surely born in the United States, but were they subject to its jurisdiction in the sense of "[n]ot owing allegiance to anybody else"? Senator Trumbull noted that "[t]he provision . . . that 'all persons born in the United States, and subject to the jurisdiction thereof, are citizens'. . . means subject to the complete jurisdiction thereof." Trumbull proceeded to deny that Indians were "in any sense subject to the complete jurisdiction of the United States. . . . We make treaties with them, and therefore they are not subject to our jurisdiction. . . . It cannot be said of any Indian who owes allegiance, partial allegiance if you please, to some other Government that he is 'subject to the jurisdiction of the United States'."

The author of the citizenship clause, Senator Howard, emphatically agreed with Trumbull's assessment that Indians would not become citizens of the United States as a result of the passage of the Fourteenth Amendment:

> the word "jurisdiction," as here employed, ought to be construed so as to imply a full and complete jurisdiction on the part of the United States, coextensive in all respects with the constitutional power of the United States, whether exercised by Congress, by the executive, or by the judicial department; that is to say, the same jurisdiction in extent and quality as applies to every citizen of the United States now. Certain, gentlemen cannot contend that an Indian belonging to a tribe, although born within the limits of a state, is subject to this full and complete jurisdiction.

Clearly, insofar as Indians owed tribal allegiance they were not within the jurisdiction of the United States, even though they were born within its territorial limits and in many instances subject to its laws. It is important to note here that jurisdiction does not mean simply subject to the laws of the United States. Rather, it refers specifically to *"political jurisdiction"* in the sense of allegiance. Aliens in the United States are properly subject to the laws of the United States and the jurisdiction of its courts; but this is not the same as owing allegiance to the United States. Aliens subject to the laws of the United States still

WHICH COUNTRIES GRANT BIRTHRIGHT CITIZENSHIP?

Country	Birth*	Notes
Australia	No	Children of immigrants born in Australia are citizens
Canada	Yes	Children born to foreign parents after February 1977 are citizens at birth
France	No	A child of foreign-born parents must apply and be approved for citizenship
Germany	No	Those born in Germany automatically acquire the citizenship status of their mother
Israel	No	If Jewish, a child is automatically a citizen; otherwise, must be the child of an Israeli National to be a citizen
Italy	No	One parent must be Italian
Japan	No	One parent must be a citizen of Japan
Norway	No	One parent must be Norwegian
Philippines	No	One parent must be a citizen of the Philippines
Poland	No	One parent must be Polish
Republic of Korea	No	One parent must be a citizen of Korea
Spain	Yes	However, the child needs one year of residence to become a citizen if the parents are foreigners
Sweden	No	If mother is Swedish, the child acquires citizenship at birth; if parents are resident aliens, the children acquire the citizenship of their parents
Switzerland	No	If child was born before June 1, 1985, the father must be Swiss for the child to be a Swiss citizen; if the child is born after June 1, 1985, the child will be a Swiss citizen if either parent is Swiss
Taiwan	No	One parent must be a citizen of Taiwan
United Kingdom	No	One parent must be a citizen or a legal resident of the UK for the child to be a citizen

*"Birth" refers only to whether or not a person is guaranteed citizenship simply by being born in that country. However, excluded from consideration are the children of diplomats, or other persons on official government business in a foreign country.

Center for Immigration Studies, September 1993.

owe allegiance to another country and are thus not within the political jurisdiction of the United States—the only jurisdiction contemplated by the Fourteenth Amendment. . . .

As the Supreme Court said in Elk v. Wilkins (1884), "[t]he evident meaning of [the jurisdiction clause] is, not merely subject in some respect or degree to the jurisdiction of the United States, but completely subject to their political jurisdiction and owing them direct and immediate allegiance. . . . Indians, born within the territorial limits of the United States, members of and owing immediate allegiance to one of the Indian Tribes, an alien though dependent power, although in a geographical sense born in the United States, are no more 'born in the United States and subject to the jurisdiction thereof,'. . . than the children of subjects of any foreign government born within the domain of that government; or the children, born within the United States, of ambassadors or other public ministers of foreign Nations." In this case, Elk had renounced his tribal allegiance and had lived for some years apart from the tribe. But the Court was adamant that the ascription of citizenship could not be a unilateral or self-selected act. "The alien and dependent condition of the members of the Indian Tribes could not be put off at their own will, without the action or assent of the United States" signified either by treaty or legislation. Neither "the Indian Tribes" nor "individual members of those Tribes," no more than "other foreigners" can "become citizens of their own will." It must be emphasized that no individual can be made a citizen against his will or consent. Yet, self-selected citizenship is not enough; it must be ratified by those [who] are already members of the political community.

The Supreme Court in Elk noted that several congressional acts had been passed subsequent to the Fourteenth Amendment to bring various Indian tribes within the jurisdiction of the United States, acts "which would have been superfluous if they were or might become, without an action of the government, citizens of the United States." In this regard, the Court mentions the "Act of July 15, 1870," extending the jurisdiction of the United States to any member of the Winnebago tribe who desired to become a citizen. A similar act was passed on March 3, 1873, extending jurisdiction to members of the Miami tribe of Kansas. Indeed, this was the method used by Congress—exercising its Section 5 powers to enforce the provisions of the Fourteenth Amendment—to bring various members of Indian tribes within the jurisdiction of the United States. General legislation was passed in the Indian Citizenship Act of 1924 which provided that "all non-citizen Indians born within the territorial limits of the United States be, and they are hereby, declared to be citizens of the United States." Thus, Congress has a long history of exercising its Section 5 powers to define who fall within the jurisdiction of the United States.

WHAT STATUS FOR CHILDREN OF ILLEGAL ALIENS?

In the case of the children born to aliens illegally in the United States, their citizenship would follow the citizenship of their parents—or be determined by the laws of the country in which the parents hold citizenship. The fact that illegal aliens have violated laws of the United States precludes any possibility that they can be properly said to be within the jurisdiction of the United States as the aliens surely have demonstrated that they do not believe themselves to be subject to the laws of the United States, or are only partially subject. Contrary to a currently fashionable argument, the denial of birth-right citizenship to children of illegal aliens does not punish the children for the sins of the parents because the children don't have a right to citizenship in the first place—they are being denied nothing that is rightfully theirs. It would, of course, be a different matter for the children born of legal aliens who have been admitted by the laws of the United States. Whether their children would be citizens at birth or upon the attainment of citizenship by the parents would be a matter for Congress to determine.

Congress, of course, has plenary power, under terms of Article I, Section 8 of the Constitution "to establish an uniform Rule of Naturalization." By necessary inference, Congress has the power to regulate immigration and set the terms by which those who are legally admitted can remain in the country. It certainly can establish the standards for which the contract of citizenship can be offered and the qualifications of those to whom it will be proffered. I believe that Congress is fully competent, under the Fourteenth Amendment, to pass legislation defining those who are "subject to the jurisdiction" of the United States. It does not require a constitutional amendment to withhold citizenship from children born in the United States of illegal alien parents. Their parents are not "subject to the jurisdiction" of the United States and they seek citizenship for their children without the consent of the nation. It defies logic to insist that an illegal act on the part of parents can confer the boon of citizenship upon their children. The nation has specified the terms of its consent in the uniform rules for naturalization and laws governing immigration.

The argument for birth-right citizenship is, of course, more suitable to feudalism than it is to republicanism. Under the feudal concept of citizenship, anyone born under the protection of the sovereign owed perpetual allegiance or fealty to the sovereign. It is hardly credible that the framers of the American Constitution would have contemplated a basis for citizenship that had its origins in the feudal regime. Indeed, in basing citizenship on the consent of the governed, the obligations of citizenship were placed on an entirely new—and republican—basis. The Reconstruction Congress recognized this point when it passed the Expatriation Act of 1868. This act—a companion piece to the Fourteenth Amendment—was an explicit rejection of birth-right citizenship as the ground for American citizenship. It simply declared that "the right of expatriation is a natural and inherent right of all people, indispensable to the enjoyment of the rights of life, liberty, and the pursuit of happiness." Thus the English common law doctrine of birth-right citizenship was decisively rejected as incompatible with the principles of consent embodied in the Declaration of Independence. Senator Howard, the author of the Fourteenth Amendment's citizenship clause, stated that those principles necessarily mean that "the right of expatriation . . . is inherent and natural in man as man. . . ." The notion of birth-right citizenship was frequently described as an "indefensible feudal doctrine of indefeasible allegiance." One member of the House of Representatives gave expression to the general sense of the Congress when he concluded that "[i]t is high time that feudalism were driven from our shores and eliminated from our law, and now is the time to declare it."

Sir William Blackstone had described the allegiance required by the English doctrine of birth-right citizenship in these terms:

> Natural allegiance is such as is due from all men born within the king's dominions immediately upon their birth. For, immediately upon their birth, they are under the king's protection. . . . Natural allegiance is therefore a debt of gratitude; which cannot be forfeited, canceled, or altered, by any change of time, place, or circumstance. . . . For it is a principle of universal law, that the natural-born subject of one prince cannot by any act of his own, no, not by swearing allegiance to another, put off or discharge his natural allegiance to the former: for this natural allegiance was intrinsic, and primitive, and antecedent to the other; and cannot be divested without the concurrence act of that prince to whom it was first due.

AN INCONSISTENT PRINCIPLE

The English common law became a part of the American system only insofar as it was consistent with the principles of republican government. Among a host of other considerations, birth-right citizenship denies that the people always retain the natural right to revolution, a right that is the fundamental right of rights described in the Declaration of Independence. As Representative Normal Buel Judd remarked on the floor of the House, "the English common law was not adopted . . . except so far as applicable to our situation and our form of government. . . . The very origin and nature of our institutions utterly forbid the idea that the doctrine of 'perpetual allegiance' is consistent with our institutions." Representative Judd further specified the precise sense in which the common law doctrine of birth-right citizenship was inconsistent with the principles of "our institutions": "The right of expatriation is clearly implied as inalienable in the enumeration of rights in the Declaration of Independence, and its obstruction was one of the wrongs charged by the colonies against the English crown." There can be no doubt whatsoever that the fortieth Congress that passed the Expatriation Act believed that it contained a thoroughgoing repudiation of the English common law notion of birth-right citizenship and its attendant requirement of perpetual allegiance. Since this Act was contemporaneous with the adoption of the Fourteenth Amendment, there can be little doubt that it also embraced the principle of citizenship that was embodied in the amendment. Reciprocal consent is the principle of citizenship embraced in the Fourteenth Amendment and the Expatriation Act is a confirmation of that principle.

Chief Justice Melville Weston Fuller remarked in his dissenting opinion in United States v. Wong Kim Ark (1898) that in the American Revolution "when the sovereignty of the Crown was thrown off and an independent government established, every rule of the common law and every statute of England obtaining in the colonies, in derogation of the principles on which the new government was founded, was abrogated." It was emphatically the case, Fuller rightly argued, "that the rule making locality of birth the criterion of citizenship because creating a permanent tie of allegiance, no more survived the American Revolution than the same rule survived the French Revolution." Indeed, the consensual basis of citizenship, so far from creating a permanent and indissoluble allegiance to the sovereign, maintains "the general right of expatriation, to be exercised in subordination to the public interests and subject to regulation."

The majority decision in Wong Kim Ark failed to make an adequate case for American adoption of the English common law basis of citizenship. Wong Kim Ark's parents were legal residents of the United States but were rendered ineligible for citizenship by both statutes and treaty; and they still maintained their allegiance to China. The Court nevertheless held—wrongly in my view—that Wong Kim Ark, having been born within the territorial limits of the United States, had birth-right citizenship. The majority opinion failed to see that the English common law of birth-right citizenship was not only contrary to the principles of the founding, but had been explicitly rejected by the Fourteenth Amendment and the Expatriation Act. In any case, there has never been a Supreme Court opinion holding that the children of *illegal aliens* are entitled to American citizenship by virtue of their birth within the geographical limits of the United States.

"The [Fourteenth] amendment's
purpose was to remove the right of
citizenship by birth from transitory
political pressures."

THE UNITED STATES SHOULD NOT
REPEAL BIRTHRIGHT CITIZENSHIP

Walter Dellinger

Walter Dellinger is an assistant attorney general in the Office of
Legal Counsel in the Justice Department. The following viewpoint is Dellinger's testimony at a joint hearing before the
House Subcommittee on Immigration and Claims and the Subcommittee on the Constitution of the Committee on the Judiciary. Dellinger argues that the Fourteenth Amendment, which
grants citizenship to all babies born in the United States whether
their mothers are legal or illegal residents, is a fundamental part
of America's constitutional heritage and should not be changed.
The straightforward language of the amendment, he asserts, re-
sists the influence of politics and social trends. Denying birth-
right citizenship to certain classes of people is beyond the authority of Congress, he maintains.

As you read, consider the following questions:

1. What is Dellinger's interpretation of the phrase "subject to
   the jurisdiction thereof"?
2. What was the Supreme Court's decision in *Wong Kim Ark*,
   according to the author?
3. In Dellinger's opinion, why would it be a grave mistake to
   change the Fourteenth Amendment?

Reprinted from Walter Dellinger's congressional testimony in *Societal and Legal Issues Surrounding
the Children Born in the United States to Illegal Alien Parents*, a joint hearing before the Subcommittee
on Immigration and Claims and the Subcommittee on the Constitution, Committee on the
Judiciary, House of Representatives, 104th Cong., 1st sess., December 13, 1995.

Throughout this country's history, the fundamental legal principle governing citizenship has been that birth within the territorial limits of the United States confers United States citizenship. The Constitution itself rests on this principle of the common law. As Justice Noah Swayne wrote in one of the first judicial decisions interpreting the Civil Rights Act of 1866, the word "'Citizens' under our constitution and laws means free inhabitants born within the United States or naturalized under the laws of Congress. We find no warrant for the opinion that this great principle of the common law has ever been changed in the United States." When Justice Swayne wrote these words, the nation was only beginning to recover from a great Civil War sparked in no small part by the Supreme Court's tragically misguided decision in the *Dred Scott v. Sanford* case. That decision sought to modify the founders' rule of citizenship by denying American citizenship to a class of persons born within the United States. In response to *Dred Scott* and to the Civil War, Congress enacted the 1866 Act, and Congress and the States adopted the Fourteenth Amendment in order to place the right to citizenship based on birth within the jurisdiction of the United States beyond question. Any restriction on that right contradicts both the Fourteenth Amendment and the underlying principle that the amendment safeguards. . . .

THE CONSTITUTION IS THE LAW

Because the rule of citizenship acquired by birth within the United States is the law of the Constitution, it cannot be changed through legislation, but only by amending the Constitution. A bill . . . that purports to deny citizenship by birth to persons born within the jurisdiction of this country is unconstitutional on its face. Second, . . . constitutional amendments on this topic conflict with basic constitutional principles. To adopt such an amendment would not be technically unlawful, but it would flatly contradict our constitutional history and our constitutional traditions. Affirming the citizenship of African-Americans that *Dred Scott* had denied, in 1862 President Abraham Lincoln's attorney general wrote an opinion for the secretary of the treasury asserting "[a]s far as I know . . . you and I have no better title to the citizenship which we enjoy than the 'accident of birth'—the fact that we happened to be born in the United States." Today, in 1995, we cannot and should not try to solve the difficult problems illegal immigration poses by denying citizenship to persons whose claim to be recognized as Americans rests on the same constitutional footing as that of any natural-born citizen. . . .

The Fourteenth Amendment declares that "All persons born or naturalized in the United States, and subject to the jurisdiction thereof, are citizens of the United States and of the State wherein they reside." The unmistakable purpose of this provision was to constitutionalize the existing Anglo-American common law rule of jus soli or citizenship by place of birth and especially to extend it to persons of African descent and their descendants.

The phrase "subject to the jurisdiction thereof" was meant to reflect the existing common law exception for discrete sets of persons who were deemed subject to a foreign sovereign and immune from U.S. laws, principally children born in the United States of foreign diplomats, with the single additional exception of children of members of Indian tribes. Apart from these extremely limited exceptions, there can be no question that children born in the United States of aliens are subject to the full jurisdiction of the United States. And, as consistently recognized by courts and attorneys general for over a century, most notably by the Supreme Court in *United States v. Wong Kim Ark*, there is no question that they possess constitutional citizenship under the Fourteenth Amendment.

THE QUALIFICATIONS FOR CITIZENSHIP

While the Constitution recognized citizenship of the United States in prescribing the qualifications for president, senators, and representatives, it contained no definition of citizenship until the adoption of the Fourteenth Amendment in 1868. Prior to that time, citizenship by birth was regulated by common law. And the common law conferred citizenship upon all persons born within the territory of the United States, whether children of citizens or aliens. The only common law exceptions to this generally applicable rule of jus soli were children born under three circumstances—to foreign diplomats, on foreign ships, and to hostile occupying forces—which, under principles of international law, were deemed not to be within the sovereignty of the territory.

As the legislative history of the Civil Rights Act of 1866 and the Fourteenth Amendment makes clear, the definitions of citizenship contained in both were intended to codify the common law and overrule *Dred Scott*'s denial of citizenship to persons of African descent. Thus, with the three limited exceptions already noted and the additional exception of tribal Indians, the Fourteenth Amendment guaranteed citizenship to all persons born in the United States, including children born to aliens.

The Civil Rights Act of 1866 provides that "[A]ll persons

born in the United States, and not subject to any foreign power, excluding Indians not taxed, are hereby declared to be citizens of the United States." During the debates on the Act, the Chair of the House Judiciary Committee stated that the provision defining citizenship is "merely declaratory of what the law now is," and he cited, among other authorities, a quotation from William Rawle, whose constitutional law treatise was one of the most widely respected antebellum works: "Every person born within the United States, its Territories or districts, whether the parents are citizens or aliens, is a natural-born citizen in the sense of the Constitution, and entitled to all the rights and privileges appertaining to that capacity."

The Fourteenth Amendment initially contained no definition of citizenship. Senator Jacob Howard of Michigan proposed to insert the definition that became the opening sentence of the Fourteenth Amendment:

"This amendment which I have offered is simply declaratory of what I regard as the law of the land already, that every person born within the limits of the United States, and subject to their jurisdiction, is by virtue of natural law and national law a citizen of the United States."

He explained that this was not meant to include those discrete classes of persons excluded by the common law, "but will include every other class of persons."

ALIENS AND CITIZENSHIP

The Framers intended the amendment to resolve not only the status of African-Americans and their descendants, but members of other alien groups as well. This is reflected in the exchange between Senators Lyman Trumbull and John Conness, supporters of the Fourteenth Amendment and the Civil Rights Act, and Senator Edgar Cowan, a strong opponent of both. Senator Cowan expressed his reluctance to amend the Constitution in such a way as would "tie the[ ] hands" of the Pacific states "so as to prevent them from [later] dealing with [the Chinese] as in their wisdom they see fit." The supporters of the citizenship clause responded by confirming their intent to constitutionalize the U.S. citizenship of children born in the United States to alien parents.

Senator Cowan. "I am really desirous to have a legal definition of 'citizenship of the United States.' What does it mean? . . . Is the child of the Chinese immigrant in California a citizen? Is the child of a gypsy born in Pennsylvania a citizen?"

Senator Conness. "The proposition before us . . . relates . . . to the children begotten of Chinese parents in California, and it is proposed to declare that they shall be citizens. We have declared that by law; now it is proposed to incorporate the same provision in the fundamental instrument of the nation. I am in favor of doing so."

THE SUPREME COURT RECOGNIZES BIRTHRIGHT CITIZENSHIP

The constitutional guarantee of citizenship to children born in the United States to alien parents has consistently been recognized by courts, including the Supreme Court, and attorneys general for over a century. Most notably, in *United States v. Wong Kim Ark*, the Supreme Court held that a child born in San Francisco of Chinese parents (who, under the Chinese Exclusion laws then in effect, could never themselves become U.S. citizens) became at the time of his birth in the United States a citizen of the United States, by virtue of the Fourteenth Amendment.

The Court, in a detailed review of the Anglo-American common law of citizenship and the legislative history of the Fourteenth Amendment, established several propositions. First, because the Constitution does not define United States citizenship, it must be interpreted in light of the common law. Under the common law of England, which was adopted by the United States, every child born within the territory of alien parents was a natural-born subject, with the exception of children born of foreign ambassadors, of alien enemies during hostile occupation, and of aliens on a foreign vessel.

Further, "[a]s appears upon the face of the [Fourteenth] Amendment, as well as from the history of the times, [the amendment] was not intended to impose any new restrictions upon citizenship, or to prevent any persons from becoming citizens by the fact of birth within the United States, who would thereby have become citizens according to the law existing before its adoption. It is declaratory in form, and enabling and extending in effect." Specifically, the Court explained, "[t]he real object . . . in qualifying the words '[a]ll persons born in the United States,' by the addition, 'and subject to the jurisdiction thereof,' would appear to have been to exclude, by the fewest and fittest words, (besides children of members of the Indian tribes, standing in a peculiar relation to the National Government, unknown to the common law) the two classes of cases— children born of alien enemies in hostile occupation, and children of diplomatic representatives of a foreign State—both of which . . . by the law of England, and by our own law . . . had been recognized exceptions to the fundamental rule of citizenship by birth within the country."

In concluding its review of the relevant law, the Court summarized: "The Fourteenth Amendment affirms the ancient and fundamental rule of citizenship by birth within the territory, in the allegiance and under the protection of the country, including all children here born of resident aliens, with the exceptions or qualifications (as old as the rule itself) of children of foreign sovereigns or their ministers, or born on foreign public ships, or of enemies within and during a hostile occupation of part of our territory, and with the single additional exception of children of members of the Indian tribes owing direct allegiance to their several tribes. The Amendment, in clear words and in manifest intent, includes the children born, within the territory of the United States, of all other persons, of whatever race or color, domiciled within the United States. Every citizen or subject of another country, while domiciled here, is within the allegiance and the protection, and consequently subject to the jurisdiction, of the United States."

DO NOT DIVIDE THE NATION

There are three ways to become an American—by choice, through naturalization; by blood, through having an American parent; and by birth in the United States. It is also true that most nations do not have these three methods. The simplest contrast is Germany. With very few exceptions, you can only be a German if your ancestors were German. There are hundreds of thousands of second and third generations of people, born in Germany, knowing no other nation, who are not German, who will never be German. Congress should think again whether you wish to make the United States more like Germany. . . .

Caution. There are nations in the world that have tried this, and we are not like them. We are not a nation that is permanently divided into "us" and "them.". . . The United States must not follow [this] model, where citizens are the privileged elite, and foreigners do the dirty work.

Barbara Jordan, testimony before the House Subcommittee on Immigration and Claims and the Subcommittee on the Constitution, December 13, 1995.

The Court then turned to the status of Chinese persons in the United States under the Constitution and the Chinese Exclusion Acts, which provided for exclusion and expulsion of Chinese persons. After considering the effects of both sources of law, the Court held that Wong Kim Ark had become a citizen at birth by virtue of the Fourteenth Amendment, reaffirming the constitutional principle that "[t]he Fourteenth Amendment, while it leaves the power, where it was before, in Congress, to regulate naturalization, has conferred no authority upon Congress to restrict the effect of birth, declared by the Constitution to constitute a sufficient and complete right to citizenship."

The principles set forth in *Wong Kim Ark* cannot be dismissed as having been overtaken by contemporary judicial interpretation or current events. Both the courts and commentators have consistently cited and followed the principles of *Wong Kim Ark*. . . .

BEYOND THE AUTHORITY OF CONGRESS

In short, the text and legislative history of the citizenship clause as well as consistent judicial interpretation make clear that the amendment's purpose was to remove the right of citizenship by birth from transitory political pressures. The Supreme Court noted in *Wong Kim Ark*, "[t]he same Congress, shortly afterwards, evidently—thinking it unwise, and perhaps unsafe, to leave so important a declaration of rights to depend upon an ordinary act of legislation, which might be repealed by any subsequent Congress, framed the Fourteenth Amendment of the Constitution." More recently, the Supreme Court noted in *Afroyim v. Rusk* that the framers of the Fourteenth Amendment "wanted to put citizenship beyond the power of any governmental unit to destroy." See also *Rogers v. Bellei*, 401 U.S. at 835 (recognizing that "Congress has no 'power, express or implied, to take away an American citizen's citizenship without his assent,'" where that citizenship is attained by birth). By excluding certain categories of native-born persons from U.S. citizenship, . . . legislation [to deny birthright citizenship to illegal immigrants] impermissibly rescinds citizenship rights that are guaranteed to those persons by the citizenship clause of the Fourteenth Amendment. Such a rescission of constitutionally protected rights is beyond Congress' authority.

Congress is, of course, constitutionally free to propose, and the states to ratify, any amendment to the Constitution. Such naked power undeniably exists. The Constitution taken as a whole, however, stands for certain enduring principles. When Congress undertakes to tamper through the amendment process with the most basic presuppositions of American constitutionalism, it should do so with exceeding caution and utmost restraint. The proposition that all persons born in the United States and subject to its jurisdiction are citizens at birth is one of those bedrock principles.

Academics may conceive of nation-states in which citizenship would not necessarily extend to those who lack the approval or mutual consent of existing citizens. But the country in question is not some theoretical conception, but our own country with its real experience and its real history. It would be a grave mistake to alter the opening sentence of the Fourteenth Amendment without sober reflection on how it came to be part of our basic constitutional charter.

The constitutional principle with which these proposed amendments would tamper flows from some of the deepest wellsprings of American history. From the earliest days of our nation, with the tragic exception of slaves and tribal Indians, all those who were born on its soil and subject to no foreign power became its citizens. The simple fact of birth here in America was what mattered.

A MONSTROUS MISTAKE

And then came Dred Scott. In its most monumentally erroneous decision, the Supreme Court created a monstrous exception to the common law rule that birth on American soil to a free person was sufficient for American citizenship. The Court held that no persons of African descent—including free persons of African descent—and none of their descendants for all time to come could ever be citizens of the United States regardless of their birth in America.

It was in the aftermath of this decision that one of our great political parties was formed. In 1857, in the first of many speeches he was to give on the subject, that party's candidate for President in 1860 denounced Dred Scott's creation of a class of persons born on American soil and yet without rights and condemned to pass their status on to future generations. Abraham Lincoln declared that the defenders of that decision had committed themselves to a principle that contradicted—and that made a "mere wreck, a mangled ruin" of—the Declaration of Independence.

Afterwards, the nation plunged into the heart of darkness—a savage and brutal civil war in which hundreds of thousands lost their lives on the battlefield. From those ashes, a nation was re-formed. It is no trivial matter that the Fourteenth Amendment opens with the principle that some would now change. From our experience with Dred Scott, we had learned that our country should never again trust to judges or politicians the power to deprive from a class born on our soil the right of citizenship. We believe that no discretion should be exercised by public officials on this question—there should be no inquiry into whether or not one came from the right caste, or race, or lineage, or bloodline in establishing American citizenship. Other nations may seek more consensual and perhaps more changeable forms of citizenship; for us, for our nation, the simple, objective, brightline fact of birth on American soil is fundamental.

FREE AND EQUAL CITIZENS

Since the Civil War, America has thrived as a republic of free and equal citizens. This would no longer be true if we were to amend our Constitution in a way that would create a permanent caste of aliens, generation after generation after generation born in America but never be among its citizens. To have citizenship in one's own right, by birth upon this soil, is fundamental to our liberty as we understand it. In America, a country that rejected monarchy, each person is born equal, with no curse of infirmity, and with no exalted status, arising from the circumstance of his or her parentage. All who have the fortune to be born in this land inherit the right, save by their own renunciation of it, to its freedoms and protections. Congress has the power to propose an amendment changing these basic principles. But it should hesitate long before so fundamentally altering our republic.

PERIODICAL BIBLIOGRAPHY

The following articles have been selected to supplement the diverse views presented in this chapter. Addresses are provided for periodicals not indexed in the *Readers' Guide to Periodical Literature*, the *Alternative Press Index*, the *Social Sciences Index*, or the *Index to Legal Periodicals and Books*.

George J. Borjas	"The New Economics of Immigration," *Atlantic Monthly*, November 1996.
Robert E. Burns	"Don't Slam the Lid on the Melting Pot," *U.S. Catholic*, March 1997.
Linda Chavez	"What to Do About Immigration," *Commentary*, March 1995.
Barry R. Chiswick	"Immigration Policy: The Case for Radical Reform," *Jobs & Capital*, Summer 1994. Available from 1250 Fourth St., 2nd Fl., Santa Monica, CA 90401-1353.
Commonweal	"Reform or Resentment?" January 13, 1995.
Eric Cox	"Why Harsh Immigration Laws?" *Human Quest*, January/February 1997. Available from 1074 23rd Ave. North, St. Petersburg, FL 33704.
Susan Crabtree	"Immigration Crossroads," *Insight*, March 25, 1996. Available from 3600 New York Ave. NE, Washington, DC 20002.
Alan Fechter and Michael S. Teitelbaum	"A Fresh Approach to Immigration," *Issues in Science and Technology*, Spring 1997.
Robert D. King	"Should English Be the Law?" *Atlantic Monthly*, April 1997.
Charles Pasqua	"Facing the Facts," *Harvard International Review*, Summer 1994. Available from PO Box 401, Cambridge, MA 02238.
Alejandro Portes and Min Zhou	"Should Immigrants Assimilate?" *Public Interest*, Summer 1994.
Peter D. Salins	"Assimilation, American Style," *Reason*, February 1997.

For Further Discussion

Chapter 1

1. List some of the examples Thomas L. Nichols gives of the benefits of immigration. What examples does Garrett Davis provide of the drawbacks of immigration? Whose use of examples do you find more convincing? Explain your answer.

2. According to Peter Roberts, in what ways do immigrants adversely affect America's economy? In Frank Julian Warne's opinion, how has immigration benefited the economy? Do you think Warne effectively counters Robert's argument? Why or why not?

3. John F. Kennedy, a third-generation American, maintains that immigration should not be limited by a national origins quota system. Marion Moncure Duncan, whose ancestors came to America before the Revolutionary War, asserts that such quotas are appropriate and necessary. In your opinion, how might the authors' family backgrounds affect the stances they take in their viewpoints? Do you find any actual evidence of such influence in the viewpoints?

Chapter 2

1. Yeh Ling-Ling is a naturalized U.S. citizen of Chinese descent. She argues that America will become an overcrowded and impoverished Third World nation if it continues to allow the importation of poor immigrants. What effect, if any, do you think her background has on her views? Do you agree with her reasoning? Why or why not?

2. Michael Lind asserts that America experienced its biggest economic booms during periods in which immigration was sharply restricted. He maintains that reducing the number of legal and illegal immigrants who come to the United States would protect the jobs and wages of American workers. How does Charles Lane respond to Lind's arguments? Which viewpoint is strongest, and why?

3. Frank del Olmo reports that changing conditions in Mexico will soon lower the number of illegal immigrants who come to the United States looking for work. Based on your readings of the viewpoints in this book, do you agree or disagree with his argument? Explain your answer.

CHAPTER 3

1. James Thornton contends that refusing to allow illegal aliens to receive social services, welfare benefits, and public education for their children will reduce the number of illegal immigrants to the United States. Raul Hinojosa and Peter Schey maintain, however, that these anti-illegal immigrant measures would actually harm society. Based on the viewpoints, do you think these services should be denied to illegal immigrants? Why or why not?

2. John J. Miller and Stephen Moore argue that a national identification card would give the federal government dangerous police-state powers that would have a minimal effect on illegal immigrant workers. How does Susan Martin respond to these charges? Which author makes the stronger argument? Explain your answer.

3. According to Ben J. Seeley, the U.S.-Mexico border is a war zone that needs American troops to protect it against an invasion of illegal border crossers. The *Revolutionary Worker* responds that using U.S. troops on the border threatens the lives of innocent people. Based on your reading of the viewpoints, do you think the U.S.-Mexican border should be militarized? Why or why not? Does the same argument apply to the U.S.-Canada border? Explain your answer.

CHAPTER 4

1. U.S. immigration policy allows the close and extended family members of immigrants already in the United States to receive a preference when applying for an immigration visa. Based on your readings of the viewpoints in this book, should U.S. immigration policy be changed, and if so, how? Explain your answer.

2. Walter Dellinger, an assistant attorney general of the United States, maintains that the Fourteenth Amendment guarantees U.S. citizenship to anyone born on American soil. How does Edward J. Erler, a university professor of political science, respond to Dellinger's argument? Which viewpoint is strongest, and why? Does the author's background influence your assessment of his argument? Explain.

ORGANIZATIONS TO CONTACT

The editors have compiled the following list of organizations concerned with the issues debated in this book. The descriptions are derived from materials provided by the organizations. All have publications or information available for interested readers. The list was compiled on the date of publication of the present volume; the information provided here may change. Be aware that many organizations take several weeks or longer to respond to inquiries, so allow as much time as possible.

American Civil Liberties Union (ACLU)
125 Broad St., 18th Fl., New York, NY 10004
(212) 549-2500 • fax: (212) 549-2646
web address: http://www.aclu.org

The ACLU is a national organization that works to defend Americans' civil rights guaranteed by the U.S. Constitution. The ACLU publishes and distributes policy statements, pamphlets, and the semiannual newsletter *Civil Liberties Alert*.

American Friends Service Committee (AFSC)
Immigrant and Refugee Rights Project
1501 Cherry St., Philadelphia, PA 19102
(215) 241-7134 • fax: (215) 241-7119
e-mail: Lperez@afsc.org • web address: http://www.afsc.org

AFSC is a Quaker organization committed to peace, social justice, and humanitarian service. The committee works with immigrants in the United States and abroad and monitors abuses of human and civil rights by immigration law enforcement agencies. Its numerous publications include *Sealing Our Borders: The Human Toll* and *Operation Blockade: A City Divided*. The project also has a packet of information on immigration and refugee rights available on request.

American Immigration Control Foundation (AICF)
PO Box 525, Monterey, VA 24465
(540) 468-2022 • fax: (540) 468-2024
e-mail: aicf@cfw.com • web address: http://www.cfw.com/~aicf

AICF is an independent research and education organization that believes massive immigration, especially illegal immigration, is harming America. It calls for an end to illegal immigration and for stricter controls on legal immigration. The foundation publishes the monthly newsletter *Border Watch* and the book *Immigration Out of Control: The Interests Against America*.

Americans for Immigration Control (AIC)
AIC Office
717 Second St. NE, Suite 307, Washington, DC 20002
(202) 543-3719 • fax: (202) 543-5811

AIC is a lobbying organization that works to influence Congress to adopt legal reforms that would reduce U.S. immigration. It calls for increased funding for the U.S. Border Patrol and the deployment of military forces to prevent illegal immigration. It also opposes amnesty for illegal immigrants. AIC offers articles and brochures explaining its position on immigration issues and publishes *Immigration Watch* twice a year.

Americas Watch (AW)
485 Fifth Ave., New York, NY 10017-6104
(212) 972-8400 • fax: (212) 972-0905
e-mail: hrwnyc@hrw.org • web address: http://www.hrw.org

AW, a division of Human Rights Watch, promotes human rights, especially for Latin Americans. It publicizes human rights violations and encourages international protests against governments responsible for them. AW publications include *Brutality Unchecked: Human Rights Abuses Along the U.S. Border with Mexico*.

The Brookings Institution
1775 Massachusetts Ave. NW, Washington, DC 20036
(202) 797-6000 • fax: (202) 797-6004
web address: http://www.brook.edu/

Founded in 1927, the institution is a liberal research and education organization that publishes material on economics, government, and foreign policy. It publishes analyses of immigration issues in its quarterly journal, *Brookings Review*, and in various books and reports.

Calgary Immigrant Aid Society (CIAS)
910 Seventh Ave. SW, 12th Fl., Calgary, AB
T2P 3N8, CANADA
(403) 265-1120 • fax: (403) 266-2486
e-mail: cias@cadvision.com
web address: http://www.cadvision.com/cias

CIAS works to assure immigrants the opportunity to fully participate in the Canadian community. It believes that all immigrants should be treated equally and fairly. CIAS works with government agencies, volunteers, and the community to ensure the fair treatment of immigrants. The *Calgary Immigrant Aid Society Bulletin* is the society's quarterly newsletter.

Cato Institute

1000 Massachusetts Ave. NW, Washington, DC 20001-5403
(202) 842-0200 • fax: (202) 842-3490
e-mail: cato@cato.org • web address: http://www.cato.org

The Cato Institute is a libertarian public policy research foundation dedicated to limiting the role of government and protecting individual liberties. It believes immigration is good for the U.S. economy and favors easing immigration restrictions. The institute has published Julian L. Simon's book *The Economic Consequences of Immigration*, as well as various articles on immigration.

Center for Immigration Studies

1522 K St. NW, Suite 820, Washington, DC 20005
(202) 466-8185 • fax: (202) 466-8076
e-mail: center@cis.org • web address: http://www.cis.org/cis

The center researches and analyzes the social, economic, environmental, and demographic effects of immigration on America. Among its numerous publications on immigration is the quarterly journal *Immigration Review*.

Federation for American Immigration Reform (FAIR)

1666 Connecticut Ave. NW, #400, Washington, DC 20009
(202) 328-7004 • fax: (202) 387-3447
e-mail: fair@fairus.org • web address: http://www.fairus.org

FAIR works to stop illegal immigration and to limit legal immigration. It believes that the growing flood of immigrants into the United States causes higher unemployment and drains social services. FAIR publishes the monthly newsletter *FAIR Immigration Report* and the bimonthly *FAIR Information Exchange* as well as many reports and position papers.

National Council of La Raza (NCLR)

1111 19th St. NW, Suite 1000, Washington, DC 20036
(202) 785-1670 • fax: (202) 776-1792

NCLR is a national organization that seeks to improve opportunities for Americans of Hispanic descent. It conducts research on many issues, including immigration, and opposes restrictive immigration laws. The council publishes and distributes congressional testimonies and reports, including *Unlocking the Golden Door: Hispanics and the Citizenship Process*, and the quarterly newsletter *Agenda*.

National Immigration Forum

220 I St. NE, Suite 220, Washington, DC 20002-4362
(202) 544-0004 • fax: (202) 544-1905
web address: http://www.immigrationforum.org

The forum believes legal immigrants strengthen America and that welfare benefits do not attract illegal immigrants. It supports effective measures aimed at curbing illegal immigration and promotes programs and policies that help refugees and immigrants assimilate into American society. The forum publishes the quarterly newsletter *Golden Door* and the bimonthly newsletter *Immigration Policy Matters*.

National Network for Immigrant and Refugee Rights (NNIRR)
310 Eighth St., Suite 307, Oakland, CA 94607-4253
(510) 465-1984 • fax: (510) 465-1885
e-mail: nnirr@nnirr.org • web address: http://www.nnirr.org

The network includes community, church, labor, and legal groups committed to the cause of equal rights for all immigrants. These groups work to end discrimination against and unfair treatment of illegal immigrants and refugees. The network aims to strengthen and coordinate educational efforts among immigration advocates nationwide. It publishes a quarterly newsletter, *Network News*.

Negative Population Growth, Inc. (NPG)
1608 20th St. NW, Suite 200, Washington, DC 20009
(202) 667-8950 • fax: (202) 667-8953
e-mail: npg@npg.org • web address: http://www.npg.org

NPG believes that world population must be reduced and that the United States is already overpopulated. It calls for an end to illegal immigration and an annual cap on legal immigration of 200,000 people. This would achieve "zero net migration" because, according to NPG, 200,000 people exit the country each year. NPG frequently publishes position papers on population and immigration in its *NPG Forums*.

Ontario Council of Agencies Serving Immigrants (OCASI)
110 Eglinton Ave. West, 2nd Fl., Toronto, ON M4R 1A3, CANADA
(416) 322-4950 • fax: (416) 322-8084
e-mail: ocasi1@web.net • web address: http://www.web.net/~ocasi1

OCASI acts as a collective voice for the over one hundred community-based organizations in the province of Ontario who work to improve services and programs for immigrants and refugees. OCASI works to achieve equality, access, and full participation for immigrants and refugees in every aspect of Canadian life. It believes that immigrants and refugees are vital to the Canadian economy and are not a financial burden on society. It publishes the quarterly *OCASI Newsletter* and the *OCASI Monthly Report* as well as various policy and resource papers.

The Rockford Institute
934 N. Main St., Rockford, IL 61103-7061
(815) 964-5053 • fax: (815) 965-1827

The institute is a conservative research center that studies capitalism, religion, and liberty. It has published numerous articles questioning immigration and legalization policies in its monthly magazine *Chronicles*.

U.S. Border Patrol
Immigration and Naturalization West Regional Office
web address: http://www.ins.usdoj.gob

The Border Patrol is the mobile uniformed enforcement arm of the Immigration and Naturalization Service. The agency's mission is to maintain control of the international boundaries between ports of entry by detecting and preventing the smuggling and unlawful entry of immigrants into the United States. It publishes various brochures, including *Operation Gatekeeper: Landmark Progress at the Border*.

BIBLIOGRAPHY OF BOOKS

Brent Ashabranner — *Our Beckoning Borders: Illegal Immigration to America.* New York: Cobblehill, 1996.

Roy Howard Beck — *The Case Against Immigration: The Moral, Economic, Social, and Environmental Reasons for Reducing U.S. Immigration Back to Traditional Levels.* New York: W.W. Norton, 1996.

Vernon M. Briggs Jr. — *Mass Immigration and the National Interest.* Armonk, NY: M.E. Sharpe, 1996.

Peter Brimelow — *Alien Nation: Common Sense About America's Immigration Disaster.* New York: Random House, 1995.

Leon F. Bouvier and Lindsey Grant — *How Many Americans? Population, Immigration, and the Environment.* San Francisco: Sierra Club Books, 1994.

Peter Morton Coan — *Ellis Island Interviews: In Their Own Words.* New York: Facts On File, 1997.

Wayne A. Cornelius, Philip L. Martin, and James F. Hollifield — *Controlling Immigration: A Global Perspective.* Stanford, CA: Stanford University Press, 1994.

Vic Cox — *The Challenge of Immigration.* Hillside, NJ: Enslow, 1995.

Peter Duignan and Lewis H. Gann, eds. — *The Debate in the United States over Immigration.* Stanford, CA: Hoover Institute Press, 1997.

Timothy J. Dunn — *The Militarization of the U.S.-Mexico Border, 1978–1992: Low Intensity Conflict Doctrine Comes Home.* Austin: University of Texas Press, 1996.

Richard M. Ebeling and Jacob G. Hornberger, eds. — *The Case for Free Trade and Open Immigration.* Fairfax, VA: Future of Freedom Foundation, 1995.

Georgie Anne Geyer — *Americans No More.* New York: Atlantic Monthly Press, 1996.

Maryann Jacobi Gray, Elizabeth Rolph, and Elan Melamid — *Immigration and Higher Education: Institutional Responses to Changing Demographics.* Santa Monica, CA: RAND, 1996.

David G. Gutierrez, ed. — *Between Two Worlds: Mexican Immigrants in the United States.* Wilmington, DE: Scholarly Resources, 1996.

Darrell Y. Hamamoto and Rodolfo D. Torres, eds. — *New American Destinies: A Reader in Contemporary Asian and Latino Immigration.* New York: Routledge, 1996.

Nigel Harris	*The New Untouchables: Immigration and the New World Worker.* New York: St. Martin's Press, 1995.
David M. Heer	*Immigration in America's Future: Social Science Findings and the Policy Debate.* Boulder, CO: Westview Press, 1996.
David A. Hollinger	*Postethnic America: Beyond Multiculturalism.* New York: BasicBooks, 1995.
John Isbister	*The Immigration Debate: Remaking America.* West Hartford, CT: Kumarian Press, 1996.
David Jacobson	*Rights Across Borders: Immigration and the Decline of Citizenship.* Baltimore: Johns Hopkins University Press, 1998.
Peter Kwong	*Forbidden Workers: Illegal Chinese Immigrants and American Labor.* New York: New Press, 1998.
Louise Lamphere, Alex Stepick, and Guillermo Grenier	*Newcomers in the Workplace: Immigrants and the Restructuring of the U.S. Economy.* Philadelphia: Temple University Press, 1994.
Gerald Leinwand	*American Immigration: Should the Open Door Be Closed?* New York: Franklin Watts, 1995.
Michael Lind	*The Next American Nation: The New Nationalism and the Fourth American Revolution.* New York: Free Press, 1996.
Stephen C. Loveless et al.	*Immigration and Its Impact on American Cities.* Westport, CT: Praeger, 1996.
Wayne Lutton and John Tanton	*The Immigration Invasion.* Petoskey, MI: Social Contract Press, 1994.
Dale Maharidge	*The Coming White Minority: California's Eruptions and America's Future.* New York: Times Books, 1996.
Joel Millman	*The Other Americans: How Immigrants Renew Our Country, Our Economy, and Our Values.* New York: Viking Press, 1997.
Nicolaus Mills, ed.	*Arguing Immigration: The Debate over the Changing Face of America.* New York: Simon and Schuster, 1994.
Laurie Olsen	*Made in America: Immigrant Students in Our Public Schools.* New York: New Press, 1997.
Silvia Pedraza and Ruben G. Rumbaut, eds.	*Origins and Destinies: Immigration, Race, and Ethnicity in America.* Belmont, CA: Wadsworth, 1996.
Juan F. Perea, ed.	*Immigrants Out! The New Nativism and the Anti-Immigrant Impulse in the United States.* New York: New York University Press, 1997.
Alejandro Portes and Ruben G. Rumbaut	*Immigrant America: A Portrait.* Berkeley: University of California Press, 1996.

Robert Royal, ed. *Reinventing the American People: Unity and Diversity Today.* Grand Rapids, MI: Eerdmans, 1995.

Peter D. Salins *Assimilation, American Style.* New York: BasicBooks, 1997.

Lucy E. Salyer *Laws Harsh as Tigers: Chinese Immigrants and the Shaping of Modern Immigration Law.* Chapel Hill: University of North Carolina Press, 1995.

Paul J. Smith, ed. *Human Smuggling: Chinese Migrant Trafficking and the Challenge to America's Immigration Tradition.* Washington, DC: Center for Strategic and International Studies, 1997.

Thomas Sowell *Migrations and Cultures: A World View.* New York: Basic-Books, 1996.

Michael Tonry *Ethnicity, Crime, and Immigration: Comparative and Cross-National Perspectives.* Chicago: University of Chicago Press, 1997.

Sanford J. Ungar *Fresh Blood: The New American Immigrants.* New York: Simon and Schuster, 1995.

Chilton Williamson *The Immigration Mystique: America's False Conscience.* New York: BasicBooks, 1996.

Norman L. Zucker and Naomi Flink Zucker *Desperate Crossings: Seeking Refuge in America.* Armonk, NY: M.E. Sharpe, 1996.

INDEX